The Scarborough

Part 1: The Old Town

The site of Newborough Bar. The white three storey building on the right was the residence of William 'Strata' Smith between 1835 and 1839

Front Cover:
St Mary's Street - early 1900s

Rear Cover:
Dumple Street looking up from the Market prior to demolition in the 1930s, now Friargate

CONTENTS

INTRODUCTION

The history of the seaside is effectively mirrored in the history and heritage of Scarborough. Many of the buildings that you will see on the Scarborough Heritage Trail represent milestones on this long and eventful journey from obscure fishing village to thriving seaside town. From the mid 17th century onwards, the far-spreading fame of the medicinal Spa waters brought the rich, the well-connected and the fashionable to Scarborough every season. Much earlier than anywhere else, too, sea bathing became an acceptable feature of the 'Scarborough Experience'. These discerning early visitors sought pleasure as well as health. They demanded - and were prepared to pay for - the best of everything, from accommodation, food and drink to theatrical performances, elegant balls and banquets.

By following the Heritage Trail, you will be able to trace some of the development in the social, religious, literary and artistic life of the rapidly growing town, and the buildings associated with each sphere of activity.

The Heritage Trail also provides a glimpse or two of the earlier medieval walled town, when the narrow streets were thronged with cowled monks and friars as well as with the European seafarers and traders attracted to the busy port for the trade outlets it offered. Later, during the 18th and early 19th centuries, shipbuilding vied in importance with holidaymaking as a major source of economic growth. Here too, the Heritage Trail gives you an insight into the great days of sail as well as of the men who built and owned the ocean-going wooden vessels.

Places, events and people described in this booklet represent a necessarily selective choice of historic sites, mostly located in or near what is now called the 'Old Town', where the traditional fishing community first established itself before the Norman Conquest. Fishing remains a feature of the local economy today.

A second book, Heritage Trail Part 2, covers South Cliff and Spa, Crescent and Town Centre and North Bay.

Suggestions for further reading are given on page 27.

A street map, obtainable from the Information Centres, will be of help in the location of all places mentioned in this booklet.

1 The Grand Hotel

With the arrival of the railway in 1845, Scarborough was well placed to attract a wider spectrum of visitors than ever before. They came now to savour the new-found delights of an established seaside resort, rather than to sample the medicinal Spa waters. The wealthier and more sophisticated of these visitors, who demanded a standard of accommodation and cuisine not hitherto available, were rewarded with a hotel that excelled any other throughout Europe at that time, either in situation, size or range of amenities. Its lofty and spacious ground floor lounge still retains some of the aura of a more expansive age.

The locally funded Scarborough Cliff Hotel Company engaged the well-known architect, Cuthbert Brodrick, who designed Leeds Town Hall, Leeds Corn Exchange and the Town Hall at Hull, to design a magnificent building on 12 floors and with 365 rooms, towering 160 feet above the sea. The St. Nicholas Cliff site alone cost the company £30,000.

In 1865, with the hotel less than half completed, the Scarborough Cliff Hotel Company went into liquidation. A Leeds businessman, Archibald Neil, bought both site and building at auction for the knock-down price of £43,000. Work then went ahead once more, still to the original plans of Cuthbert Brodrick. By 1867, the Grand Hotel was ready for occupation and was reputed to be the largest and most advanced hotel in Europe.

With its four distinctive domes (representing the seasons of the year), it still dominates the South Bay seafront. It has survived bombardment by the German fleet in December 1914, several changes of ownership and as many financial crises.

The Grand Hotel has adapted to cater for 21st century visitors and remains one of Scarborough's main attractions. A Grade II* listed building.

The Grand Hotel, once the largest hotel in all Europe, still dominates Scarborough's South Bay skyline

2 Anne Brontë

Scarborough held a special appeal for Anne Brontë, youngest of the three famous Brontë sisters. She made three or four visits, and it was here that she chose to come from her Haworth home in the final stages of her fatal illness (tuberculosis). Thanks to a legacy of £200 from her godmother, Anne could afford to stay at her favourite lodgings in the fashionable St. Nicholas Cliff area - on a site where the Grand Hotel now stands - and to pay the expenses of her elder sister, Charlotte, as well as Charlotte's old school friend, Ellen Nussey. (They were charged 30 shillings a week each for their lodgings).

The three of them arrived at No. 2, The Cliff on 25th May 1849, where Anne was able to enjoy for the last time the incomparable views. Within three days, she was dead. Because St. Mary's Parish Church was undergoing restoration at the time, Anne's funeral service was held at nearby Christ Church in Vernon Road (close to the present public library) which was demolished in 1979.

Anne Brontë's grave in St. Mary's churchyard

Ellen Nussey registered Anne's death and mistakenly entered her age as 28, instead of 29, an error not since rectified on the tombstone in St. Mary's churchyard (see page 24). Charlotte complained later about this and other errors in the inscription. The local Civic Society has erected a commemorative plaque to Anne Brontë next to the main entrance of the Grand Hotel near where No.2 The Cliff once stood.

As Acton Bell, Anne Brontë wrote two novels – 'The Tenant of Wildfell Hall' and 'Agnes Grey'. She also left us 59 poems, which are perhaps her greatest gift to posterity.

No more than 100 yards from the Grand Hotel you will find Scarborough's oldest hotel, the Royal, on St. Nicholas Street, well-known to 18th century visitors as the Long Room.

2a The Central Tramway

The Central Tramway runs between the town centre on Marine Parade (at the North side of The Grand Hotel) and the beach at Foreshore Road in the South Bay and is still owned and operated by the same corporate entity that established the Tramway in 1881. The attractive top station is an excellent example of Victorian design which enhances its primary function of carrying the Scarborough public and visiting holiday makers between the town centre and the beach. The amenity is a credit to Victorian engineering, much of which remains intact today.

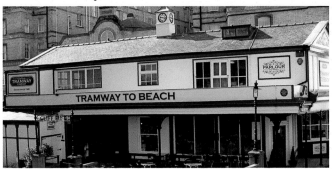

3 The Long Room and Royal Hotel

Assembly Rooms or Long Rooms were at the heart of entertainment and social life in Spa resorts and Scarborough was no exception. The first Long Rooms were on Sandside and Princess Street. By 1725, a more sumptuous Long Room had been established at the seaward end of St. Nicholas Street (which was then called Long Room Street). Reputedly designed by the Earl of Burlington, who had earlier planned the Assembly Rooms at York, this new Long Room boasted an 'Egyptian Hall', 112 feet long, 40 feet wide and 40 feet high. This massive room was the elegant setting for the Grand Balls held regularly during the 18th century seasons. You could also dine in some style, and play billiards and card games. In effect, the Long Room was an upper class nonresidential social club for Scarborough's well heeled visitors. In 1733 it cost five shillings a year to join and one shilling for an evening attendance. The present day Royal Hotel ballroom may incorporate some of the fabric of the 18th century Long Room.

The Long Room was purchased by a Mr. Edward Donner towards the turn of the century, and became popularly known as 'Donner's Rooms' to early 19th century visitors. It seems that Donner added bedrooms to the building in the 1820s still incorporating the original Long Room. He sold out around 1840 and the Royal Hotel begins to be mentioned from this time onwards. Edward Donner's former house in St. Nicholas Street was absorbed into the hotel in 1847, and a new block by the architect Henry Wyatt was added on the Harcourt Place frontage in 1862. The present day dining room was constructed in 1935 on a site formerly occupied by the billiards room.

The Royal's entrance hall and main staircase, in the oldest part of the building, provide a reminder of the elegance of a bygone age. For 30 years, from 1935, the hotel was owned and managed by the Laughton family. The late Mr. Tom Laughton purchased and hung many paintings by major artists in the public rooms. (Some of these paintings are included in the Tom Laughton Collection at Scarborough Art Gallery, at the far end of The Crescent).

The Royal Hotel stands on the site of the former Long Room,
the fashionable hub of Scarborough's social life during the 18th century seasons

The Royal Hotel is a Grade II listed building. In 2013 there were over 1960 listed items in the Borough of Scarborough, including 26 Grade I and 86 grade II* buildings.

Queen Victoria's Statue in the Town Hall Gardens. Once the private home of a prominent local banker, the Jacobean-style Town Hall was purchased by Scarborough Corporation in 1898.

4 The Town Hall (formerly St. Nicholas House)

The Town Hall, just across the street from the Royal Hotel, was built in the 1840s as a residence for John Woodall, a member of a prominent family of Scarborough bankers. The building was designed by Henry Wyatt who displayed the design at the Royal Academy in 1852. Wyatt also designed the 'Gothic Pavilion' at the Spa and Woodall, Hebden & Co's bank at the corner of St Nicholas Street and Newborough – now Barclays. The style of the house is Jacobean in red brick with stone trim and this style was emulated when the building was acquired by Scarborough Corporation and substantially enlarged and remodelled to form the Town Hall. The original owner's initials may be seen in the gable end high above the main entrance which also contains the ornate date 1844.

John Woodall died on 9th February 1879 and was succeeded by his son John W. Woodall, who offered the house and associated gardens to the Corporation in 1898. The decision as to where to site a new Town Hall was resolved at a meeting on 5th April 1898, when the Corporation decided to buy St. Nicholas House. Harry W. Smith, the recently appointed borough engineer and surveyor, designed the new eastern (seaward) wing in a similar style to the original, to accommodate the council chamber and other offices. The Jacobean theme was continued in the design of the Council chamber and other features. This work was completed in 1903 and the new Town Hall was officially opened by Princess Henry of Battenburg in the same year.

The purchase also included the St Nicholas Cliff undercliff and the Borough Engineer also redesigned these gardens which were opened to the public on 14th August 1900. Further redesign and substantial remodelling was done in 2001 and the gardens were reopened on the 12th December of that year. Harry Smith went on to lay out or redesign most of Scarborough's parks and pleasure grounds during the next 30 years, including Peasholm Park and the Italian Gardens on the South Cliff. Further alterations to the Town Hall were made in 1962-64, with extensions in King Street and St. Nicholas Street.

The statue of Queen Victoria in the Town Hall gardens is the only statue of a public figure to be found in Scarborough.

5 Theakston's Bookshop

Walking a few yards further along St. Nicholas Street brings you to Solomon Theakston's former bookshop at No. 31, now an entrance to Marks and Spencer's store. Theakston was a 19th century Scarborough 'institution', well patronised by both residents and visitors during his period of ownership from 1841 to 1875. He was neither the first nor the only bookseller in town, but certainly ended up as the best known. Theakston, a native of York, opened a library and bookshop across the street at No. 6 in 1828. He transferred the expanding business to larger premises on the other side at No. 31 in 1841.

The move enabled him to house not only his wife and himself, but also an amazing variety of enterprises behind the Georgian façade of the building, which had originally been a lodging house. From 1845 onwards, he printed and published on the premises the weekly 'Scarborough Gazette', with its accompanying list of visitors, as well as a popular guide book to the town which ran into many editions between 1840 and 1881. In addition to the library and bookshop, he set up a fine arts gallery, where H. B. Carter, a celebrated painter of local scenes and seascapes, exhibited and sold many of his works. Tickets for the Spa Theatre were on sale at Theakston's; you could also buy wallpaper there, and even arrange to collect your mail at No. 31.

When Solomon Theakston died childless in 1875, aged 64, his former clerk, John Haygard, continued all the business activities until 1895. The Theakston 'empire' then went gradually into decline and was ultimately acquired by W. H. Smith and Son Limited. From 1904 W. H. Smith's traded as booksellers and stationers at the premises until moving to a new purpose-built shop on Westborough in 1981.

The site was then purchased by Marks and Spencer and incorporated in a major store extension. The present St. Nicholas Street frontage is a replica of the late 18th century building. Marks and Spencer gained a local Civic Society award for this work.

When you reach the end of St Nicholas Street, turn left on to the Newborough pedestrian precinct and walk as far as North Street. This marks the historic site of the original Newborough Bar.

6 Newborough Bar

From medieval times, Scarborough was a walled and moated town. Newborough Bar was the centrepiece of these fortifications and the principal point of entry. It was probably erected before the reign of Henry III and was rebuilt in 1642. Newborough Bar also served as a local prison for several centuries, refractory and drunken prisoners being confined on the north side of the bar, debtors on the south side next to the gaoler's lodgings.

It was last fortified in 1745, when 6 guns were mounted on either side of Newborough Bar. The guns were never fired in action, and the bar reverted to its penal function for the next 100 years. When the prisoners were transferred to more secure and less insanitary premises, first in Castle Road and then to the 'model' prison in Dean Road designed by the architect W. B. Stewart and built in 1866 (still surviving in a different role), Newborough Bar had outlived its useful purpose.

It was demolished in 1847 and replaced by the purely ornamental Newborough Bar, designed by John Barry. This imposing neo-Gothic castellated structure impeded the growing traffic flow along the town's main street. It was bought by the Corporation in 1890 and knocked down.

At the end of North Street the building that stands next to the site of Newborough Bar was formerly the Bar Hotel. On the wall of this building can be found a plaque along with a fixture for the Pancake Bell (dated 1996). The bell, which is placed in situ on Shrove Tuesday, is rung to start the annual pancake race. This bell is a comparatively new edition of the original 'curfew' bell.

Now retrace your steps down the Newborough pedestrian precinct and turn left on to St Thomas Street. Just before Chapman, Preston & Hastie's (CPH) estate agency on the right stood a famous theatre for nearly 200 years.

7 Theatre Royal

Scarborough can claim one of the longest theatrical traditions of any town in the country outside London. When the old Theatre Royal on Tanner (now St. Thomas) Street closed in 1924, it marked the end of approaching 200 years of theatrical performances on that site. A guide book of 1734 refers to the theatre (then no more than a tented booth) as an already established feature, with a Mr. Kerregan bringing a theatrical company from York 'every season'. After taking the Spa waters in the morning, the nobility and gentry liked to while away the afternoon at the theatre. Later, they took a leisurely stroll back down Long Room (St. Nicholas) Street to dine, dance and gamble the night away at the Assembly Rooms (see page 5).

One of the several owner-managers was Stephen George Kemble, brother of the celebrated Mrs. Siddons, who performed at the Theatre Royal, with all the other theatrical 'greats' of the 19th century. Visitors could expect to see famous names like Charles Kemble, Edmund Kean, William Charles MacReady and Ellen Terry topping the bill. Earlier, in 1781, the playwright Sheridan had written a comedy entitled 'A Trip to Scarborough'.

As the number of visitors increased during the 19th century, the compact 18th century theatre became too small to cope. Henry Mayhew, the enterprising owner-manager between 1886 and 1919, enlarged the building considerably in the 1880s to accommodate audiences of over 1,000. The theatre survived somewhat precariously until 1924.

Later, the building was purchased by Scarborough

9

Corporation and was demolished under a road-widening scheme.

Nothing remains today to remind the passer-by of this 200 year old Thespian tradition, and only a dwindling band of older Scarborians can now recall the final years of the old Theatre Royal.

Retrace your steps to Newborough, and turn left down this hilly road leading to the Old Town area. The second road on your right is Bland's Cliff. Walk a few yards down this steep and narrow cobbled street until you reach the Bell Hotel, set back on the right of Bland's Cliff.

8 Formerly The Bell Inn

There has been an inn, known first as the Blue Bell Inn, near the top of the serpentine Bland's Cliff since at least 1776. Later, as the Bell Hotel, it was one of Scarborough's principal coaching inns.

The Bell not only accommodated those who came to sample the Spa waters but was also the station for the prestigious daily Royal Mail coach to York, among other regular coaching services. When the railways overtook the horse-drawn coaches, the nobility and gentry had already moved elsewhere to seek their pleasures, and the Bell was forced to adjust to changing circumstances. In 1839, the 'commercial gentlemen' who serviced the expanding town's many trade outlets, could obtain full board – with 'mountains' of food included – for six shillings a day.

One such distinguished guest was Dr Granville, the celebrated 'Spa traveller'.

As the 19th century progressed, holidaymakers also helped to fill the hotel's bedrooms right up to the late 1930s.

A reminder of the bustling coaching days can still be found in the adjacent Prospect Place. Note the clipped brickwork on the end wall of No. 7, where careless coachmen sometimes misjudged the distance. Together, the four-square Bell Hotel and Prospect Place make up a unique 18th century enclave on the edge of the Old Town area.

Another former coaching inn (now flats and offices) was the Talbot Hotel, 14 Queen Street. You will pass it on the way back to town at the end of the Heritage Walk.

Returning now to Newborough, cross the street and enter St. Helen's Square, which is almost opposite Bland's Cliff. You can now see the massive proportions of the 19th century Market Hall on the right-hand side.

Although built in 1853, the Market Hall is still a pleasing feature of St. Helen's Square and remains a busy shopping centre

9 Market Hall

Before the construction of the Market Hall in 1853, weekly markets were held in various parts of Scarborough, each often associated with one commodity. For example, Newborough was the Thursday Market, at which pots, glass and earthenware goods were on sale from Bar Street down to St. Nicholas Street; and stalls of general goods on both sides of the street further down to St. Helen's Square. On Saturdays, a market was held in Princess Street.

The new Market Hall was built by a private market company and opened on 8th August 1853. Annual Street fairs were still held, however, at Martinmas and Whitsuntide, with the tolls now passing to the market company. An Order of the Home Secretary in November 1896 terminated all the surviving annual fairs held in Newborough. The market company was paid £300 compensation by the Corporation for loss of all these tolls. One street market – that of the

11

corn merchants - persisted in nearby King Street until the 1950s, however.

The market building was designed by John Irvin, Borough Surveyor (who died less than three months before it opened) and cost £16,000. Despite its down-to-earth purpose, it is a dignified building with pleasing lines, mercifully unmodified since erection. The two decorative borough seals on the front elevation possess a special charm.

Scarborough Fair, now celebrated in the song popularised by Simon and Garfunkel, flourished for over 500 years. Between 15th August and 29th September every year, the annual herring fish fair was held mainly on the sands. It also extended to the narrow streets and alehouses of the Old Town which were crowded with local tradesmen and European merchants, as well as minstrels, fortune tellers, quack doctors and dentists, and many others. Scarborough Fair had faded into history by the end of the 18th century and was last held in 1778, though still very much alive in local folklore.

Walk now to the rear of the Market Hall - either along the adjacent Market Way or through the Market Hall itself - and you are at the top of St. Sepulchre Street. About 200 yards down this street on your right is Trinity House. It can be identified by the superior stone facing and the lettering across the width of the façade at second-storey level.

10 Trinity House

One of the properties in Scarborough designated as a Grade II* listed building (the star denotes a particularly important building), Trinity House has played a significant role in the seafaring life of the town. It is one of only four such establishments in the country, the others are at London, Hull and Newcastle-upon-Tyne, and its foundation reflects the importance of Scarborough as a port in the early 17th century. The original Society of Ship Owners and Master Mariners (35 of the former and 39 ships' captains) built almshouses on the St. Sepulchre Street site, and

First erected in 1602 and re-built in 1832 Trinity House was once the centre of Scarborough's maritime trade

later bought the land itself for £100 in 1665. A gift, left by Admiral Sir John Lawson (circa 1616 to 1665) in his will to the poor of Scarborough, funded the erection of the first Trinity House. It contained 27 apartments for aged or maimed seamen and/or their widows, as well as 'two fine rooms' in which the trustees could hold their meetings. These trustees had to be either ship-owners, master mariners or naval officers, a requirement which still applies today.

An Act of Parliament of 1747 created a merchant seamen's fund to finance such charitable institutions, financed by a levy of 6d (2½ pence) a month from all persons employed on any vessel belonging to the four ports involved. During the five-year period from 1747 to 1752, over £1,000 was raised locally by the levy – an enormous sum in those days. This fund financed the construction of the Merchant Seaman's Hospital opened in 1752 on the site of the current fire station. Even Scarborough Corporation found it convenient to borrow money from Trinity House!

In this building, the entire business of the port was conducted: ships were bought and sold in the impressive first-floor board room that remains a notable feature of the interior, cargoes arranged, insurances effected and indentures signed.

Rebuilt in 1832 to the designs of R. H. Sharp of York, Trinity House is a fine example of classical style architecture in ashlar-faced stone. Behind this distinguished frontage are now seven, self-contained modern flats, housing retired seamen and their dependants. The historic board room is lit by three chandeliers given by the Belfast descendants of Edward Harland (of Harland and Woolf fame) who, as a schoolboy, watched 'splendid East Indiamen of some 1,000 tons burden' being built at Scarborough shipyards of the Tindall family (see page 20). This boardroom, with its numerous maritime mementoes, is still used for the statutory bi-annual meetings of the 15 trustees.

Trinity House also controls an annexe of 18 flats on Tollergate, rebuilt in 1959, although there were seamen's almshouses on the site from 1752. Wilson's Mariners Homes on Castle Road, designed by John Barry, were founded and endowed by Richard Wilson - himself a former trustee of Trinity House - in 1836. They are typical single-storey almshouses built in the Gothic Style.

Now carry on walking down St Sepulchre Street, crossing to the left-hand side, until you come to a small garden area behind tall iron railings. This was a Quaker burial ground in front of the early 19th century meeting house built by the Quakers of the time.

11 The Old Quaker Meeting House

Quakers meetings for worship were held in Scarborough from 1651 onwards and weddings were known from 1661. Quakers would not take part in normal civil or religious wedding ceremonies. Instead, they performed their own marriages in front of witnesses and they took good care to publicise such proceedings, as an insurance against gossip. Early meetings were held in private homes and often resulted in heavy fines being imposed on the householder concerned.

George Fox, a pioneer of the movement, was imprisoned in Scarborough Castle from 1665 to 1666.

A perennial problem was the Quaker's attitude to carrying arms. Several of the Tindall shipbuilding family (see page 20) were Quakers but after the barque 'Morning Star' was scuttled by pirates in 1828, Robert Tindall ordered that henceforward all Tindall ships should be armed; as a consequence, he left the Society of Friends (Quakers).

In 1676, what was probably the second meeting house was opened in Low Conduit Street (now Princess Square). This was replaced by the St. Sepulchre Street building in 1801, which in turn was replaced by new premises in York Place in 1894. This was demolished in 1990 to make way for the Brunswick Pavilion Development. The new Quaker meeting house is located in Woodlands Drive near Scarborough General Hospital.

The St. Sepulchre Street building shows the characteristic plain exterior of such places, reflecting the Quakers' simple philosophy of life. Note the simple stones in the burial ground, with the minimum of information.

After years of neglect the building was restored and converted to residential use.

You are now on the edge of Princess Square. Proceed to its far right-hand corner, and turn into West Sandgate, where you will find the remnants of the historic Butter Cross, protected by a formidable circlet of iron railings.

GRAND
HOTEL
START OF
WALK.

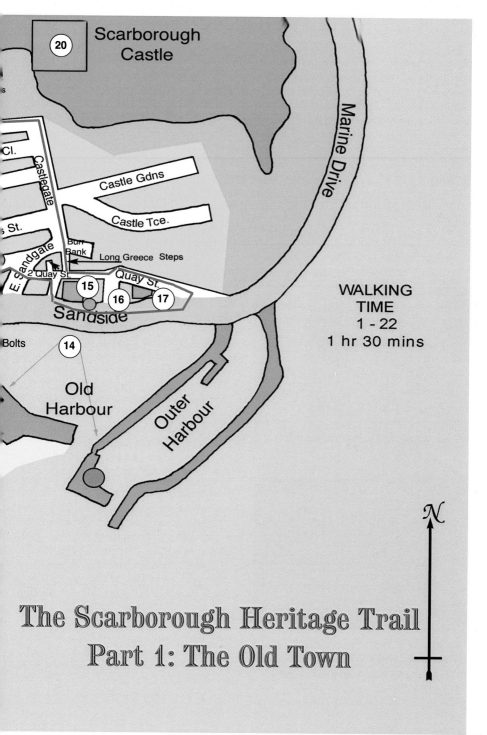

Scarborough
Castle

20

CI.

Castlegate

Castle Gdns

Castle Tce.

s St.

Burr
Bank

Sandgate

Long Greece Steps

2 Quay St.

Quay St.

15

16

17

Sandside

Bolts

14

Old
Harbour

Outer
Harbour

Marine Drive

WALKING
TIME
1 - 22
1 hr 30 mins

N

The Scarborough Heritage Trail
Part 1: The Old Town

12 The Butter Cross

Unlike many other historic towns, Scarborough lost its medieval street markets in the 1850s when the purpose-built market hall in St Helen's Square was opened. There were at least five crosses within the medieval town including the Corn Cross and Rede Cross, several of which were sited in market areas, while others may indicate the sites of markets that we no longer know about.

One of the medieval street markets in the Old Borough was located in what is now Princess Square. This Square is a wide section of street which begins at the junction of St Sepulchre Street and Cook's Row and extends as far as St Mary's Street. It was the site of the Saturday market in the 19th century but a Butter Cross has stood here since at least the 14th century which means that the origins of this street market are in the medieval period. Indeed it may be that market trading began in this area before 1155 as settlement might have occurred around the nearby Chapel of the Holy Sepulchre before the main development of the town in the reign of Henry II.

The Butter Cross in Princess Square is Scarborough's only surviving market cross. Although called a cross what actually survives is a badly eroded stone pillar with traces of crocketed leaves carved on the sides. It is thought that it is a re-used pinnacle from a church rather than part of a purpose made cross. It was probably taken from one of the friary churches after they were dissolved in 1539 or from the nearby Chapel of the Holy Sepulchre which was demolished in 1561 and was used to replace the medieval original. It has been suggested that such salvage might have been in part a symbolic act which preserved a link with one of these vanished religious buildings

Opposite the remnants of the Butter Cross is perhaps the most visually attractive public house in Scarborough still surviving. The Leeds Hotel was built in 1693 and restored with careful attention to detail in 1900 to a design by Frank A. Tugwell. Note the elaborate woodwork finish to the upper storey and the pleasing inn sign at ground floor level, lettered in Art Nouveau style.

The Butter Cross is not in its original location, nor is it the original medieval cross. However for several centuries it was the focal point of a street market

From West Sandgate, where both the Butter Cross and the Leeds Hotel are situated, carry on downhill the few yards to busy Eastborough. You should look now for a narrow alleyway on your left, which is signposted by its ancient name of The Bolts.

16

13 The Bolts

Surviving relics of medieval town life are as hard to come by in Scarborough as anywhere else. There is one unique feature, however, still existing just behind the seafront razzmatazz of modern Sandside to remind us of that long vanished world. The Bolts are a series of narrow, poorly lit passageways running intermittently behind the seafront cafés and amusement arcades.

In 1225, Henry III made a grant of forty oaks to construct a new quay and houses were erected on the new won land, however, the existence of long established rights of way ensured that the The Bolts did not disappear beneath the new buildings.

The Bolts looking east towards East Sandgate

Emerging from The Bolts at the beginning of Quay Street, the old house at the junction with Whitehead Hill (No. 2 Quay Street) is another survivor from an earlier age. It probably dates from the late 15th century and is a timber-framed gabled building with huge posts at each corner rising to the eaves. Internally they support heavy beams known as dragon beams. The timbers of the second storey jut out to support the gable but originally they supported another whole storey which would have been jettied out. No 2. Quay Street was restored in 1965; the casement windows date from then and the lath and plaster was removed at that time to reveal the timber frame. The pebbledash finish is also modern but the house still provides a reminder of how this ancient street looked in Elizabethan times, when it was the principal thoroughfare of Scarborough.

After this glimpse of Quay Street from Whitehead Hill, turn right and walk the few yards down to the harbour area on the seafront.

In addition to the dark blue 'Heritage Trail' plaques, you may see lighter blue plaques around the town, marking Scarborough's connections with notable people. There are plaques to Sir George Cayley (Paradise) Wilfred Owen (Clifton Hotel), H B Carter (York Place), Charles Laughton (West Square), Sir Edward Harland (Newborough - Marks & Spencer), William 'Strata' Smith (Newborough/Bar Street), Lord Leighton (Brunswick Centre), Sir Edwin Cooper (Nelson Street), Anne Brontë (Grand Hotel), the Sitwells (Woodend), Thomas Hinderwell (Harcourt Place), Harry W Smith (41 Westbourne Grove), Stephen Joseph (Library Vernon Road), Sachererell Sitwell (5 Belvoir Terrace), James Paul Moody (17 Granville Road).

14 The Harbour, Piers and Lighthouse

Since earliest recorded time, Scarborough's livelihood depended on the safe haven provided by the curve of sandy beach protected by the vast bulk of the Castle headland. Successive English Kings made grants for harbour works from 1225 onwards, recognising the strategic importance of a strong maritime base. King Richard III, a frequent visitor to Scarborough both before and during his short reign (see page 19) stationed warships in the port. These were the forerunners of the modern fishery protection service, and they took part in the first 'cod war' with Iceland as long ago as 1484.

During the 15th and 16th centuries, the port went into a decline. Only the fishing fleet and the transport of sea-coal kept it alive. Queen Elizabeth I granted £500, one hundred tons of timber and six tons of iron for the strengthening of the outer pier. It was severely damaged in the great storm of 1613 and subsequently repaired and maintained out of sea-coal money granted in

1614. William Vincent was responsible for an extension to the old pier and this was completed in 1752. From this date work began on the 1380 foot long East Pier which cost £12,000 and was not completed until 1826. The massive stones used in its construction, weighing up to 30 tons apiece, were quarried locally and positioned manually. Convicts were among those employed on this massive project. Smeaton's design has withstood North Sea gales since the early 19th century.

The West Pier was begun shortly afterwards, using stone from the then redundant inner island pier. The inner pier was finally demolished in 1880. All the fishing activity of the modern port, including a daily fish market is now concentrated on the West Pier. Here you will see the local cobles and larger keel-boats off-loading their catches and taking on fresh supplies. The North Wharf, adjoining Sandside, was built in 1926, when the herring trade was approaching its

The 'Coronia' pleasure boat entering Scarborough Harbour

zenith. In those colourful days, Scottish fisher lasses came South in their hundreds to gut, fillet and pack in tubs the rich herring harvest of the North Sea. It is said that you could walk across the inner harbour from end to end across the decks of the tightly packed fishing trawlers.

In 1804, the first recorded lighthouse on Vincent's Pier consisted of a flat roofed building with a brazier on top as the only warning signal. The purpose of the lighthouse at this time was to warn ships of the available depth of water in the harbour. Tallow candles, oil lamps and gas were used successively to provide a better light. The engineer Robert Nixon built a brick lighthouse at the harbour in 1806. By 1850, the lighthouse had acquired a second storey and its familiar domed top. Modern electric lighting gives a visibility of nine miles for the powerful beam. During the 1914 German Bombardment, a shell sliced through the lighthouse tower. It had to be dismantled to first floor level, and was rebuilt by public subscription in 1931.

As ships increased in both size and numbers built during the late 18th century, there were far more shipwrecks around our coasts during stormy weather, many of them happening in sight of a safe harbour. These tragedies led to the development of a lifeboat service. Scarborough's first lifeboat station was on the foreshore, near the present underground car park at the approach road to the Spa. Thomas Hinderwell, Scarborough's first serious historian, helped to secure the town's first lifeboat. Scarborough was the second place in England to have a lifeboat. The station was moved to the harbour area in 1821, firstly on the landward side of the present Foreshore Road, and latterly on the seaward side. From 1801 to 2012, there have been 1458 launches of the Scarborough Lifeboat and 577 lives saved. A total of 16 lifeboatmen were lost during this period. The worst loss of life to the lifeboat crew since the last war was when the lifeboat overturned approaching the harbour on 8th December 1954, and three crewmen were swept overboard and drowned.

Strolling along Sandside in the direction of the Castle and Marine Drive, you will come across an old stone building, known as King Richard III's house, now used as a restaurant.

15 King Richard III House

Richard Plantagenet is reputed to have stayed at this house on Sandside when he was Lord High Admiral to his brother, King Edward IV. When he became king, Richard III radically reorganised our sea defences and is credited with being the founder of the English navy in the modern sense. By this time, he was living in Scarborough Castle on his visits to the town. When the 'Navy of the North' was based at Scarborough Harbour, Richard apparently took command of the fleet at least once, when it was engaged in naval warfare with the Scottish Fleet. He granted a wide-ranging charter to Scarborough during his short reign (1483-85).

Richard III house is a very distinctive stone building which has a complex history. Much of what we see today is probably the partial survival of a much larger 17th century hall house; note the stone mullioned window in the side elevation. However part of the structure especially at ground floor level may be 15th century; this may be a house which was owned by Thomas Sage in the 1480s. The three storey bay window was built in 1912; it is a replica of a 17th century feature which had been removed in the 19th century.

Inside King Richard III's house, the principal feature worthy of note is the 17th century decorative plaster ceiling in the upper room known as the King's bedchamber. Its motifs include bulls, parrots, two sea serpents (or dolphins) and 'three hare' symbols. The

King Richard III House on Sandside

centrepiece is thought to be the rose of York – Richard's family emblem.

There was a shipyard in front of King Richard III's house during the 18th and 19th centuries and many others in both directions in the days when shipbuilding was important locally. All traces of the shipyards, the numerous slipways and the associated warehouses and chandlers' stores have vanished.

Continue along Sandside towards the Castle & Marine Drive until you pass the Golden Ball.

16 Shipbuilding in Scarborough

John Cockerill and his brother James had slipways on the Scarborough waterfront during the middle and late 17th century. The Cockerills were a well-established shipbuilding family, who intermarried with the Tindall family and eventually the two concerns became amalgamated. Seven generations of Tindalls were involved in shipbuilding, finishing with Richard who died in 1862, after which the yard was closed. Smaller boats were still built in the harbour by other yards until 1885.

The busiest period for the Tindall yards was between 1771-1800, under the direction of John Tindall (1755-1809), when 100 vessels were built. Then, shipyards lined the waterfront from Bland's Cliff to Old Pier. One of the Tindall yards was adjacent to the Old Pier; another was in front of King Richard III's house. Many of the warehouses and workshops associated with

shipbuilding were lost firstly with the completion of Foreshore Road in 1877 and later in the clearing of the old Sandside area in 1902.

Paintings in Scarborough Art Gallery by H. B. Carter, Ernest Dade and Atkinson Grimshaw, among others, convey an excellent impression of the local maritime scene during the 19th century.

When iron and steel replaced wood in ship construction, Scarborough faded quite rapidly from the shipbuilding scene and from shipowning, too.

Continue along Sandside until you reach the roundabout at the beginning of the Marine Drive. Turn sharp left into Quay Street and walk along this quaint and narrow street until you reach the Three Mariners Inn on your left.

17 The Three Mariners Inn

Arguably the earliest licensed premises in Scarborough (though the Newcastle Packet on nearby Sandside is a rival claimant) the Three Mariners is certainly one of the oldest buildings in town. In the west gable end you can see an A shaped frame in massive timbers with a central post known as a crown post. This timber frame dates from the 15th century. If you look carefully you can see that many of the timbers have the roman numeral V carved into them; this is the frame number. Frames numbered VI and VII were found within the building when it was being restored a few years ago.

The Quay Street façade was re-fronted in brick in the 17th century in a style known as Artisan Mannerism. Note the external decoration: four pediments (chevrons in moulded brick) above the windows and doors, a moulded string course and the two elliptical blind windows at the end. The building was altered again in the 18th century when the ground floor windows were replaced by vertical sliding sashes and the nice doorcase and door were installed.

Because of the frame numbering, we now know that The Three Mariners is part of a much larger building. The former Dog & Duck, another 15th century timber framed building just along the street, is thought to be part of the same building but the section between the two was removed many years ago. The Old Dog and Duck has some carving known as 'brattishing' similar to 15th century buildings in York – it may have been done by the same carpenter.

The Three Mariners was once known as 'The Blockmaker's Arms', a name which suggests an association with the great shipbuilding era of later years. During Victorian times, it was a favoured haunt for the many artists who found the nearby harbour area an endless source of inspiration. For many years in the 20th century it was a museum during which time the figurehead above the side entrance was installed. After extensive restoration the building is now a private house.

Be prepared next for a fairly stiff climb up the slopes of Castle Hill. Continue along Quay Street until a flight of steps can be seen on open space to the right. Ascend Long Greece Steps and carry on up Castlegate until the road turns to the left. Paradise House is the large grey painted building on your left.

The Three Mariners Inn is probably the earliest licensed house in town. Note the 15th century timber framework in the end wall and try to spot the roman numeral V

Paradise House: looking towards the Castle

18 Paradise House

'Paradise' in medieval times meant a monastic walled garden, which is just what the 12th century French Cistercian monks created on the sloping site below and to the east of St. Mary's Church. When Henry IV ended that association in 1405, by giving custody of the parish church to Bridlington Priory, little is known about subsequent development of the Paradise site. By 1690, however, John Cockerill (see page 20), was living there in a substantial gabled house built in the Jacobean style. A century later, Paradise House and its tree-lined garden were notorious as the haunt of smugglers. An observant chronicler, William Hutton, writes in 1803 of ' a deep draw well, covered by a small outhouse' behind Paradise, which had a 'room of considerable magnitude hollowed out of the rock'. It was here that 'a nest of smugglers' outwitted the excisemen by depositing their illicit goods in what was private property. Sir George Cayley, 'the Father of Aeronautics', is widely believed to have been born here in 1773, but Cayley himself later claimed Long Room

(St. Nicholas) Street as his birthplace.

In 1856, Paradise House resumed its shipbuilding connections when young Richard Tindall set up home there. The Tindalls were by now related to the Cockerills by marriage and the two businesses had merged. East Mount, as the property was renamed by Richard Tindall, remained in the family's ownership until the First World War. Struck by a shell in the German Bombardment of 1914, the building and grounds were purchased by Christopher Colborne Graham, Mayor of Scarborough from 1913 to 1919. Mr. Graham gave the property to the Council's Education Committee, who reopened Paradise House as the Graham Sea Training School in 1917. Thus it remained for the next 55 years, training several generations of local fishermen and merchant seamen in the art and science of seamanship. The building has now been converted to flats.

Ahead of you at the end of Paradise, the parish church of St. Mary's is now clearly visible.

19 St. Mary's Parish Church

No building in Scarborough has a longer or more turbulent history than the 800-year old parish church of St. Mary's near the top of Castle Road. A church has probably occupied this commanding position even before the first castle was erected. The first single aisled structure of around 1150 was enlarged in 1180 by the addition of a west front and towers and the creation of north and south aisles. Around 1457, St. Mary's was almost doubled in size with the building of a great perpendicular aisled choir.

During the Civil War, nearly 200 years later, St. Mary's was used by the parliamentarians as a forward position for bombarding the castle. Inevitably, the castle batteries returned the fire, destroying the beautiful medieval choir and north transept. The church steeple and bells collapsed in 1659, 14 years after the bombardment. Within 10 years, enough money had been raised both nationally and locally to repair and rebuild the nave, St. Nicholas aisle

and the central tower. The western and central parts of St. Mary's were thus restored to approximately their pre-1450 dimensions, but the north transept and medieval choir have never been rebuilt.

Almost 200 years passed before further major restoration, by Ewan Christian, took place between 1848 and 1850. The numerous wooden galleries and box pews that had for long cluttered the interior were removed and the building regained some of its earlier spaciousness. The four belfry bells were replaced by a peal of eight, augmented in 1979 by two smaller bells from Christ Church in Vernon Road, a former chapel-of-ease to St. Mary's that was demolished in that year. The clock in the central tower, visible from most parts of the Old Town, was installed in 1856.

The latest important restoration of St. Mary's was undertaken in 1950, under the direction of George Pace. Since then, the Friends of St.

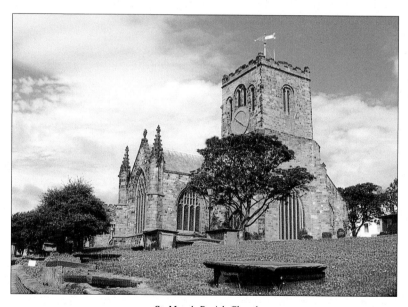

St. Mary's Parish Church

Mary's have set themselves the never-ending task of helping to preserve the fabric of this ancient parish church. On 27th September 1993, the Lady Chapel project was begun and this was completed and dedicated by John Habgood, Archbishop of York on 6th February 1994. The ruined sections of the pre-Civil War church are still visible at the eastern end of the main churchyard, silent witnesses to the fearful destruction of 1645. Beyond is the east churchyard, containing the grave of Anne Brontë (see page 5). Since the mid 19th century burials have taken place at the Dean Road Cemetery.

For students of church architecture, St. Mary's contains some odd features in the differing pillars in the nave. Some interesting medieval heads are to be seen at various vantage points in the church. Only four of the many former chantry chapels, dating from the end of the 14th century, remain today. They all lead off the south aisle.

Look out on your way up to the Castle for a weatherbeaten sandstone plaque on the garden wall of The Towers, the large battlemented house that is the last building before the Castle fortifications. This plaque commemorates the

The Hinderwell Monument, formerly sited at the junction between Castle Road and Church Lane, accidently demolished by a vehicle and nothing remains

Hinderwell Memorial Drinking Fountain of 1860, which formerly stood in the roadway at this point in memory of the great Scarborough historian, Thomas Hinderwell. The drinking fountain fell into disuse and was removed many years ago.

20 Scarborough Castle

Scarborough's 12th century Norman castle has a peaceful role today as a major tourist attraction, in marked contrast to its often warlike and bloodthirsty past.

English Heritage's illustrated booklet, entitled 'Scarborough Castle', is recommended. It is on sale at the Castle entrance.

As you repass The Towers on the way back down Castle Road, turn right by the curious little castellated lodge house on to Mulgrave Place. At the end of this short street are curved flights of steps leading up to Castle-by-the-Sea.

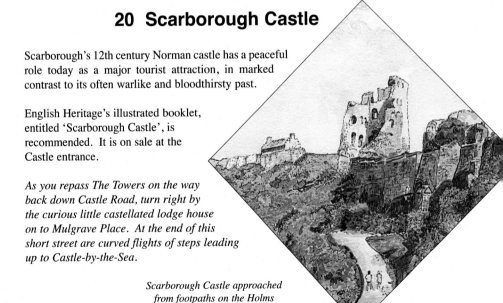

Scarborough Castle approached from footpaths on the Holms

21 Atkinson Grimshaw at Castle-by-the-Sea

Of the many talented artists attracted to the scenic beauties of the Scarborough coastline, none enjoys such a national and international reputation as John Atkinson Grimshaw, who lived with his wife and family at Castle-by-the-Sea on Mulgrave Place from 1876-79.

Grimshaw's popularity, both in his lifetime and again today, was based on the evocative 'moonlight' paintings which he perfected during his Scarborough years. His principal local patron and landlord was a wealthy retired brewer, Thomas Jarvis, who lived in The Towers, facing Castle Road. Castle-by-the-Sea, Grimshaw's seaside bungalow home, is to the rear of his patron's more substantial property.

Perhaps the most significant memento of Atkinson Grimshaw's four year residence at Castle-by-the-Sea is the lofty and spacious central room (the dining room of the present-day guest house) with its top-lit glass roof, clearly designed with an artist's requirements in mind. The massive carved mantelpiece in this room and unique tiled fireplace surround – reputedly hand-painted by the artist himself – were installed during Grimshaw's occupation. He also built the curved double flight of steps leading up to the castellated bungalow, probably incorporating an elaborate stone balustrade in the 1870s, which has since disappeared. Exotic plants were grown by the artist in the conservatory – then running round three sides of the building – some of which provided pigments for his paints.

Four typical examples of Atkinson Grimshaw's Scarborough 'moonlight' paintings are in the permanent collection at Scarborough Art Gallery. Perhaps the most dramatic is 'The Burning of the Spa Saloon', painted soon after Grimshaw's arrival from Leeds in 1876. This magnificent painting is believed to include (in the foreground) portraits of Grimshaw himself, Thomas Jarvis and members of their two families.

From the north end of Mulgrave Place you can admire the view over Scarborough's North Bay and the beautiful coastline towards Ravenscar and Whitby.

Your final destination on this Heritage Walk is the site of the first Methodist chapel in Scarborough at which John Wesley himself preached during the 18th century. Retrace your route along Church Lane, between the main and east church yards of St. Mary's and at the junction with Paradise, turn right and descend the steps behind St. Mary's. This will bring you to Church Stairs Street and just above the first house on the right is approximately where this early chapel once stood.

22 John Wesley and Church Stairs Street

John Wesley, 'the Father of Methodism' was a frequent visitor to Scarborough between 1759 and 1790, making a total of 14 visits. He was particularly fond of the chapel, which local Methodists built as their first permanent meeting place on Church Stairs Street in 1772. Wesley described this building as 'the most elegant square room which we have in England', preaching to 'elegant congregations' there on four occasions between 1772 and 1790. The chapel occupied a site, which is now an extension of St. Mary's graveyard on the right of Church Stairs Street as you descend to Longwestgate, adjoining some post-war council housing.

By the 1830s, local support for Methodism had outgrown the limited facilities on Church Stairs Street and the Blacksmith's Arms, on Queen Street, was purchased for £2,000. In 1840, the first Queen Street Chapel, designed by James Simpson was erected on vacant land adjoining the Blacksmith's Arms, which was itself re-named the Castle Hotel at about this time. (The Castle Hotel has since been demolished after being damaged by fire. The site is now occupied by Blackfriars House, so called because at one time there was a Dominican Priory on this site). The chapel of 1840 was shell-damaged in the 1914 bombardment of Scarborough and then destroyed by fire a few months later. The present-day Queen Street Methodist Central Hall, by G. E. Withers, with its distinctive twin cupolas and somewhat Byzantine appearance, was built after the 1914-18 war on the same site and opened in 1923.

Wesley's own scratched inscription – 'Watch and Pray – Wesley V. D. M.' – on a small pane of glass, believed to have come from the Church Stairs Street Chapel, is in Scarborough Museums Trust Store 'Woodend' on The Crescent.

To get back to the town centre, turn right at the bottom of Church Stairs Street and proceed along Longwestgate and Friar's Way for 500 yards to the T-junction with Queen Street. Turn left here passing what was the Talbot Hotel and the Queen Street Methodist Central Hall. At Newborough turn right for town centre destinations.

Old cottages on Church Stairs Street

Suggestions for Further Reading

Baker, Joseph Brogden (1882). A History of Scarborough. Longmans, Green and Co.

Bayliss A & P (2001). Architects and Civil Engineers of Nineteenth Century Scarborough.

Bentley, Phyllis (1969). The Brontës and their World. Thames and Hudson.

Berryman, Bryan (1972). Scarborough As It Was. Hendon Publishing.

Binns, Jack (1996). "A Place of Great Importance". Scarborough in the Civil War. Carnegie, Preston.

Binns, Jack (2001). The History of Scarborough North Yorkshire. Blackthorn Press.

Crouch D & Pearson T (Eds). Medieval Scarborough. (Yorkshire Archaeological Society, Occasional Paper No 1, 2001).

Dore, Simon (1984). Moonlight on Scarborough. (Atkinson Grimshaw). Reprint of article in Country Life (July 5 1984).

Edwards, Mervyn; Editor (1966). Scarborough 966-1966. Scarborough and District Archaeological Society.

Fairlie, Gerrard & Cayley, Elizabeth (1965). The life of a Genius. Hodder & Stoughton.

Fieldhouse, Raymond & Barrett, John (1973). The Streets of Scarborough. (revised edition 2007) Scarborough and District Civic Society.

Foord, Sydney, M.M., M.B.E. (1970). Scarborough Records. Typescript copy in Scarborough Reference Library.

Gérin, Winifred (1959). Anne Brontë. Thomas Nelson.

Goodall, J.A.A. (2000). Scarborough Castle. English Heritage.

Hinderwell, Thomas (1798, 1811, 1832). The History and Antiques of Scarborough. The 1798 edition was printed by W. Blanchard, York.

Horspool, Maurice (1982, 3rd edition). The Stones of St. Mary's.

Laughton, Tom (1977). Pavilions by the Sea. The Memoirs of an Hotel Keeper. Chatto & Windus.

Lord, Genevieve W. (1984). Scarborough's Floral Heritage. Scarborough Borough Council.

Marsay, M. (1999). Bombardment.

Pearson, Trevor (2005). The Archaeology of Medieval Scarborough. Scarborough Archaeological & Historical Society

Pearson, Trevor (2009). Scarborough: A History. Phillimore

Pevsner, Sir Nikolaus (1966). The Buildings of England: Yorkshire, the North Riding. Penguin Books.

Pritchard, J. Laurence (1961). Sir George Cayley. Max Parish.

Rowntree, Arthur; Editor (1931). The History of Scarborough. J. M. Dent.

Scarborough Archaeological & Historical Society (2003). A Guide to Historic Scarborough

Whittaker, Sir Meredith (1984). The Book of Scarborough Spaw. Barracuda Books.

Many of the above publications are available in the Reference Library on Vernon Road.

The Millennium Stone 2000
in St. Mary's churchyard

The
RHODES

PAUL HARCOURT DAVIES

NEW
HOLLAND

GLOBETROTTER™

First edition published in 2002
by New Holland Publishers (UK) Ltd
London • Cape Town • Sydney • Auckland
10 9 8 7 6 5 4 3 2 1

website: www.newhollandpublishers.com

Garfield House, 86 Edgware Road
London W2 2EA
United Kingdom

80 McKenzie Street
Cape Town 8001
South Africa

14 Aquatic Drive
Frenchs Forest, NSW 2086
Australia

218 Lake Road
Northcote, Auckland
New Zealand

Distributed in the USA by
The Globe Pequot Press, Connecticut

ISBN 1 84330 297 7

Publishing Manager (UK): Simon Pooley
Publishing Manager (SA): John Loubser
Managing Editor: Thea Grobbelaar
DTP Cartographic Manager: Genené Hart
Designer: Lellyn Creamer
Cover Design: Lellyn Creamer, Nicole Engeler
Cartographer: Nicole Engeler
Proofreader: Glynne Newlands

Reproduction by Resolution (Cape Town) and
Hirt & Carter (Pty) Ltd, Cape Town
Printed and bound in Hong Kong by Sing Cheong
Printing Co. Ltd.

Although every effort has been made to ensure
that this guide is up to date and current at time
of going to print, the Publisher accepts no
responsibility or liability for any loss, injury or
inconvenience incurred by readers or travellers
using this guide.

Note:
In the transliteration of place names from Greek
to English spellings, various authors have tried
to convey Greek sounds in different ways. The
Greek gamma is not a simple 'g' but is more
gutteral or can have a 'y' sound. Thus many
different spellings are encountered. For example,
Agios meaning 'saint', and used in all church
names (e.g. Agios Georgios) can also be spelt
Aghios or Ayios. Similarly 'dh' is sometimes used
to convey the soft 'th' sound of a Greek delta –
elsewhere you might find a simple 'd'.

Photographic credits:
AA Travel Library, pages 49, 50, 54, 65, 66;
AM Photo/Alan van Gysen, page 42; **David
Alexander**, pages 40, 53; **Paul Harcourt
Davies**, pages 20, 48; **Andreas Nicola**, pages
9, 62, 80; **Photo Access**, pages 51, 52;
PB/Jeanetta Baker, pages 81, 82; **PB/Gary
Goodwin** page 41; **PictureBank Photo
Library**, page 11; **RHPL**, cover, pages 6, 72, 79;
RHPL/David Beatty, page 78; **RHPL/N.A.
Gallow** page 12; **RHPL/Michael Jenner**, pages
8, 71, 73; **RHPL/Rolf Richardson**, page 70;
RHPL /Michael Short, page 83; **RHPL /G.M
Wilkins**, pages 44; **TI/Ian Booth** page 74, 84;
TI/Nigel Bowen-Morris, pages 76, 77;
TI/Peter Murphy, page 13; **Peter Wilson**, title
page, pages 7, 10, 16, 17, 18, 19, 21, 22, 23,
24, 26, 27, 28, 29, 30, 31, 32, 33, 34, 35, 36,
37, 38, 39, 46, 64; **Zefa Pictures**, page 47.
[PB: PhotoBank; RHPL: Robert Harding Picture
Library; TI: Travel Ink]

Front Cover: Golden sands and calm waters
make Lindos Beach extremely popular in summer.
Title Page: Byzantine and Classical civilization
valued Lindos for its unrivalled position.

CONTENTS

MAKE THE MOST OF YOUR GUIDE

Reading these two pages will help you to get the most out of your guide and save you time when using it. Sites discussed in the text are cross-referenced with the cover maps – for example, the reference 'Map A–A2' refers to the Líndos Map (Map A), column A, row 2. Use the Map Plan below to quickly locate the map you need.

MAP PLAN

Outside Back Cover   Outside Front Cover

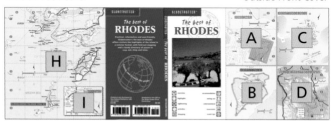

Inside Front Cover   Inside Back Cover

THE BIGGER PICTURE

<u>**Key to Map Plan**</u>

A – Líndos
B – Acropolis
C – Ancient Kámiros
D – Valley of the Butterflies
E – Rhodes
F – Rhodes Town
G – Seven Springs Area
H – Surrounding Islands
I – Kos

USING THIS BOOK

Key to Symbols

⊠ – address

☎ – telephone

〴 – fax

🖳 – website

⌁ – e-mail address

🕘 – opening times

🚌 – tour

💰 – entry fee

🍽 – restaurants nearby

Map Legend

national road	═══	main road	Makariou
main road	═══	other road	Alexandrou
minor road	═══	built-up area	
track	═══	post office	⊠
river	Plati	hotel	⒣ HERMES
city	RHODES	police station	●
large village	⊚Líndos	hospital	⊕
village	○Laérma	library	📖
peak in metres	Mt Atáviros ▲ 1215 m	place of interest	• Clock Tower
		parking	🅿
swimming	≋	place of worship	△ French Chapel
water sports	Ⓦ	tourist information	🛈
beach	⌣		
airport	✈✈	bus terminus	🚍
viewpoint	☀	park & garden	Municipal Gardens

Keep us Current

Travel information is apt to change, which is why we regularly update our guides. We'd be most grateful to receive feedback from you if you've noted something we should include in our updates. If you have any new information, please share it with us by writing to the Publishing Manager, Globetrotter, at the office nearest to you (addresses on the imprint page of this guide). The most significant contribution to each new edition will be rewarded with a free copy of the updated guide.

Above: *One of the Platóni – a bronze stag and doe that guard the entrance to Rhodes harbour.*

OVERVIEW

Rhodes is the largest in the **Dodecanese** group of islands and lies in the southeastern **Aegean Sea** some 16km (10 miles) from the Turkish coast. Its glorious coastline extends for 220km (137 miles) – most of the golden beaches are found along the limestone shores of the east; grey sands, shingle and pebble predominate on the west coast.

Tourist presence is largely concentrated in the north of the island, especially around Rhodes Town. South of Líndos (*see page 21*) and Péfkos (Péfki) it is still possible to escape crowds and, outside the main tourist season, find solitude in stunning coastal and mountain scenery. Rhodes is also an excellent base from which to begin **island-hopping**, being both a terminus for island ferry services and an important point of call on international routes to Cyprus, Israel and Egypt.

The Land
Climate

Rhodes enjoys a Mediterranean climate characterized by mild, damp winters and hot, dry summers. Rain falls in winter and early spring, from December to April. The *meltémi* blows along the west coast in summer. Beginning as a breeze at dawn, it rises to a crescendo at midday and falls towards evening.

Flora and Fauna

For much of the year, Rhodes is resplendent with seasonal **wildflowers**. Many hillsides are dotted with funeral cypress, while aleppo pine is the dominant species in forest areas.

Birdwatchers will enjoy the spring and autumn **migrations**. Moths and butterflies occur widely, as do various lizard species.

Conservation

Greece has only recently become active in conservation although some of its famous sons were writing about denudation of hills and the dangers of erosion over 2000 years ago.

The small but dedicated membership of the **Hellenic Society for the Protection of Nature** has been a relentless driving force both on the mainland and on the islands.

A society has also been formed on Rhodes to protect the remaining deer population, which is under threat from poachers.

History in Brief

Mycenaeans and Dorians

The Mycenaeans were a race from the Peloponnese mainland who exerted an influence on Rhodes. By 1500BC, they had colonized the island and established a trading empire across the eastern Mediterranean. Around 1100BC, the Dorians invaded and divided Rhodes into three city states (Líndos, Kámiros and Iálysos). In the eighth century they created the **Dorian Hexapolis**, a confederation that allied the three Rhodian cities to Kos, Knidos and Halicarnassus. This association prospered for four centuries. Rhodes flourished and established colonies in Sicily, Italy, Spain and France.

Creation of Rhodes City

In 408BC Kámiros, Líndos and Iálysos created a new capital, Rhodes City. After **Alexander the Great** occupied Kos in 336BC, the city sided with him against Persia, thus opening trade with Egypt and Syria. Following the death of Alexander in 323BC, Rhodes thwarted an attack from Demetrios Poliorketes (305–304BC), selling his siege machinery to build the **Colossus of Rhodes** as an offering to the sun god Helios.

Roman Times

In 304BC Rhodes established a pact with Rome and enjoyed unrivalled success as a commercial and naval power, until the Third Macedonian War from 171–168BC. As a result of its decision to side with King Perseus of Macedonia, Rhodes lost territories in Asia Minor, and trade was devastated when the Romans made Délos a free port in 166BC. When, in 44BC, Rhodes refused to

> **Roman Rhodes**
> Rhodes flourished under Roman rule, and by the 3rd century BC its population was more than double what it is today. The famous School of Rhetoric, founded in 342BC by Aeschines (*see page 40*), attracted a number of illustrious students, among them the young Julius Caesar. Not only was Rhodes famed as an intellectual centre, but the wares crafted by Rhodian potters and artists were also much sought-after as, indeed, they still are today (*see page 13*).

Below: *The Greeks excelled in their depiction of figures, as on this grave stele from Kámiros.*

OVERVIEW

Christian Influence
St Paul's Bay at Líndos is reputed to be where the saint landed on the island in AD51. Legend claims that Saint Paul approached Rhodes during a storm. An appeal to the Lord sent a lightning bolt that split the coastal rocks, creating a haven for the apostle to land.

The eastern Mediterranean islands played a vital role in early Christianity: Paul and his companion Barnabas visited **Cyprus** in AD47 and claimed an important convert in Governor Sergius Paulus.

support **Cassius** against his rival, Octavian (later Caesar Augustus), he vented his fury and attacked. The city was stripped of influence and fell into decline.

Age of Crusades

During the Byzantine period Rhodes was invaded on numerous occasions. The Venetians occupied the city in 1082 and nearly 200 years later, in 1261, Rhodes fell to the Genoese. In 1306 the **Knights of St John** (*see* page 44) bought Rhodes, Kos and Léros from the Genoese admiral Vignolo. By 1309 they had made it their headquarters and begun the fortifications and buildings that are, today, the great attraction of Rhodes Town.

Ottoman Turks and Italian Occupation

In 1522 Rhodes succumbed to the Ottoman ruler, **Süleyman the Magnificent**, and the Knights evacuated to Malta. Rhodes remained under Turkish rule until 1912 when the Italians seized the island following a siege. In 1943, German forces invaded. British troops liberated Rhodes in 1945 and created a transitional government. At the **Paris Peace Conference** in 1947, Greece regained control of the Dodecanese.

Post-World War II

Greece was embroiled in a civil war (1945–49) between communist and monarchist forces, won by the latter. In 1967, a CIA-backed *coup d'état* ushered in the rule of the Colonels, a military dictatorship that finally fell in 1974 after an unsuccessful invasion of Cyprus. The junta was removed and since then Greece has enjoyed democratic rule. The monarchy was abolished in 1975.

Below: *An Ottoman fountain – reminder of a Turkish rule of nearly four centuries (1522–1912).*

GOVERNMENT AND ECONOMY

Government and Economy
Government
Greeks follow politics with great avidity. Greece has enjoyed a period of relative political stability since 1974, served by a single-house parliament with 300 members. Former law professor and techno-crat, Kostas Simitis of PASOK (Pan Hellenic Socialist Movement), succeeded Andreas Papandreou as prime minister in 1996. Tension with Turkey casts a shadow over Greek politics, both in relation to Turkey's intransigence concerning the 'Cyprus question' and its refusal to recognize Greek rights to oil beneath the Aegean sea bed.

Above: *Industrious craftsmen and women have successfully adapted their skills to cater for the tourist trade.*

Economy
Along with the other members of the European Monetary Union, Greece adopted the Euro as its currency in January 2002. Tourism, seriously under threat in 1999 when the war in Yugoslavia resulted in anti-NATO demonstrations throughout Greece, is once again thriving. The industry employs more people than any other sector of the economy; even on Rhodes and the other islands it is beginning to rival the agricultural sector.

For much of the 1990s Greece's economy was dangerously feeble and, indeed, one of the weakest in Europe. Harsh measures were imposed to arrest the decline and the sacrifices successive governments imposed on the Greek people seem to have paid off: in 1999 inflation was down by 2.6%. Today, investor confidence is solid, and the stock market is, once again, booming.

Tourism
Rhodes captured the attention of the travelling public in the early 1960s. Lindos, in particular, became a popular destination for the rich and famous. While Rhodes will long continue to be a favourite tourist destination, Greece, in general, is no longer top of the list. It has suffered from the clout of large tour operators who direct their clientele to wherever they are assured a financial success. To counter this, Greece is now aiming at the 'quality' end of the market.

Above: *Goats provide milk and meat, but at the price of overgrazing.*

Agriculture

A fertile island, Rhodes has now adopted the irrigation system pioneered in Israel, permitting two harvests per year. Although the comparatively small plains make large machines impractical, cooperatives harvest crops of wheat and winter barley.

Exports of olives and wine have increased steadily, but income from agriculture has been decreasing as a whole.

Throughout Greece, the centuries-old methods of agriculture are being abandoned rather than modernized as young people make for cities and resorts. Fishing has declined in importance as catches have fallen due to over-fishing all around the Mediterranean.

The Infrastructure

Roads between ports and main centres are good. Away from the coast, they can rapidly degenerate. Public transport along the coasts is by regular bus services, but inland villages are served only by a single daily bus, if at all.

From June to September, large visitor numbers put severe strain on water supplies and sewage systems – a serious problem in view of pollution.

The People

In general, island Greeks are very friendly, but this attitude can be severely stretched in summer by the antics of holiday revellers. Locals are mostly tolerant, however, and mindful of the benefits brought by tourism. Greek males sometimes flirt with foreign female visitors – it's a game of point scoring among the men called *kámakia*. If the attention is unwanted, it pays to be polite but very firm. Rhodes is a very cosmopolitan island and women can enjoy a drink or a meal alone. For a foreign male, serious involvement with a Greek girl can still create opposition, even in the most enlightened families.

Serious crime is rare and Rhodians are swift to point out that much of the petty theft that exists is brought in by tourists.

Language

Greek, the official language of Rhodes, existed in two forms until recently: *dhimotikí* – the everyday language of ordinary folk – and *katharévoussa* – the formal language of officials (dispensed with, to the relief of many, by Andreas Papandreou). Rhodes is so geared to international tourism that all signposts are in Latin letters rather than in Greek script. Most Rhodians speak English, and many speak French or German.

If you are prepared to learn a few words of Greek (see page 91), you will find it both useful and appreciated, particularly in the villages. Remember a 'backward nod' of the head is a Greek *ochí*, meaning 'no'.

Religion

Christianity, adopted in Roman times, is promoted by the Greek Orthodox Church to which 98% of the population belongs.

The Church of Rhodes and the Dodecanese is an autonomous church headed by the Metropolitan Bishop

Women's Rights

Women in Greece and the islands did not gain the right to vote until 1956. The dominant party in Rhodes, PASOK, fought its elections in 1981 and 1985 with a strong programme for Women's Rights which included the outlawing of sexual discrimination in the workplace.

In cosmopolitan Rhodes, many women have secured university educations at home or abroad; women also run businesses and hold senior posts in the civil service. But this is still a male-dominated society where many men would consider the thought of sweeping a floor or changing a nappy emasculating. Young Rhodians are different – articulate and vocal, sexes meet here on far more equal terms.

Below: *Orthodox priests are an integral part of Greek society.*

Below: *In spite of
its attraction for
tourists, Rhodes
retains its Greek
charm and ambience.*

of Rhodes and offers its allegiance to the Patriarch of Constantinople. Priests with their dramatic black hats, long robes and full beards are shown great respect within a community – they know everyone and everything that is going on. Greeks also revere their places of worship and offence is avoided if visitors enter modestly dressed.

Myths and Legends

The founding of Rhodes gave rise to many myths. One version has it that when Zeus was apportioning the world's territories among the immortals on Mount Olympus, he over-looked the sun god, Helios. To make amends, Zeus offered him a new island which had only recently risen from the sea. Helios mar-ried Rhodos, daughter of Poseidon, and named the island in her honour.

Music

Aegean melodies have haunting cadences. Rhythms and time signatures are almost hypnotic and harken back to classical times when poetry was declaimed to the accom-paniment of a lyre. Today, village music is played on the *askómandra* or *tsamboúna* (bagpipes), *violí* (like a violin held on the knee), *klaríno* (clarinet) and *sandoúri* (hammer dulcimer).

Dance

Kalamatianó, the national dance, is a 12 step *sírto* (a slow, shuffling dance) in which a leader improvises and the rest follow, hands joined and held at shoulder level. Zorba's dance, a fea-ture of tourist entertainment at hotels, is a version of the *hasápiko* (butcher's dance). The best place to see traditional dance is at festivals or at Nelly Dimoglou Theatre in Rhodes Town (*see page 49*).

Sports

Football is a national passion. During national or international matches, the stadium in Rhodes Town is charged with an unforgettable atmosphere.

For visitors, the main attraction is the water sports offered at larger resorts throughout the island.

Above: *Designs that are centuries old are hand-painted onto ceramic items.*

Crafts and Customs

Traditional village crafts, especially ceramics, find a ready market with foreign visitors. The Rhodian plates are distinctive and make use of primary colours in strong designs: plates geared to the souvenir trade draw on mythological or historical scenes.

Art and Architecture

Rhodes has some of the finest Crusader architecture anywhere, but the Knights showed little feeling for classical or Byzantine buildings – the former were a source of stone, the latter altered as the need arose. Even so, fine Greek sculpture and architecture have survived and Byzantine religious art is evident in the frescoes and icons of some old churches. Colourful mosaic floors can be seen in the remains of Christian basilicas.

During the time of their occupation, the Italians renovated many ramshackle buildings and rebuilt parts of Rhodes Town using old plans and engravings, perhaps a little too imaginatively for some tastes.

Rhodian Pottery

Finds from tombs at Líndos, Iálysos and Kámiros have revealed much of what is known about the Minoan and Mycenaean occupation of Rhodes. Trade with Asia Minor and Egypt influenced the artists, and from the seventh century **animal motifs** were popular, as in the **Fikelloura pottery**, found near Kámiros, with its lotus flowers and partridges. Modern **plates** still make ready use of ancient designs.

13

HIGHLIGHTS

☼ See Map F   ★ ★ ★

RHODES TOWN

Rhodes Town, situated on the northern tip of the island, is without doubt one of Europe's best preserved medieval fortress towns.

Rhodes divides neatly into two quarters. The Old Town with its myriad small alleyways and magnificent historic buildings, such as the **Collachium** (see page 36), is an irresistible drawcard and a wonderful place in which to stroll. It presents an unforgettable spectacle to any visitor arriving (or returning) by boat, especially at night when spotlights pick out the massive city walls, the Ottoman minarets and the **Palace of the Grand Masters** (see page 37) located above the tranquil **Municipal Gardens** (see page 40) where an interesting nightly *Son et Lumière* recounts the fascinating tale of the Knights of St John.

Once outside the walls, the New Town offers all the wallet-emptying temptations of any cosmopolitan centre. Here, too, is bustling **Mandráki harbour** (see page 45), where the coming and going of ferries and yachts provides much to see. In the vicinity are several churches and a mosque as well as the **Aquarium of Rhodes** (see page 39).

A choice of good hotels lies within easy reach of Rhodes Town, there are some fine beaches well equipped for water sports (see pages 42–43), and the wide range of restaurants will simply delight any gastronome.

City of Rhodes Tourist Information Centre
🕑 09:00–18:00 Mon–Fri, 09:00–12:00 Sat, closed Sunday.
✉ Son et Lumière Square.
☎/📠 (0241) 35-945.

NTOG (National Tourist Office of Greece)
✉ Corner of Makaríou and Papágou streets.
☎ (0241) 23-255, or 23-655.

Son et Lumière
🕑 English performance most evenings at 20:15. For starting times and shows in other languages consult NTOG.
✉ Municipal Gardens.
🖥 www.astronet.gr/info/sound.htm

Below: *Influences of Knights and Ottomans have shaped Rhodes' Old Town.*

☼ See Map E   ★ ★ ★

WESTERN BEACHES

Below: Kremastí beach, just one of the choices along the west coast.

Just west of Rhodes Town lie the resorts that have become the island's favourite package-holiday playground. Closest is **Kritiká**, followed by **Ixiá**, which sprang up along the busy coast road that skirts the beach before moving inland at Triánda. **Triánda** (the largest settlement after Rhodes Town) boasts the island's biggest hotel complexes. Several have excellent conference facilities – **Rodos Palace** (*see page 56*), for example, has hosted an EU summit.

Kremastí, just along the coast, retained its village identity in spite of development, but visitors to **Paradíssi** should have a love of aircraft, because this village stretches virtually parallel to the airport runway – in summer, vast numbers of charter flights disgorge eager visitors to the island.

The density of the coastal development decreases as you travel west from the airport towards **Doréta beach**, near the village of **Theológos**, which (for the present) marks the end of the main holiday coast.

Getting away from it all

If solitude and relaxation are what you yearn for when you go on holiday, then the northern part of the western resorts, from Rhodes Town to Paradissi, should be avoided. This part of the coast is popular for its proximity to the island's main city and its airport. It is characterized by busy bars, eateries, hotels, apartment complexes and throngs of beachgoers in search of fun in the sun.

South of Paradíssi the atmosphere changes drastically – here you begin to feel like you are in Greece. But accommodation and restaurants become more scarce the further south you travel.

Below: Our Lady of Filérimos, the first base of the Knights.

See Map E–H3 ★ ★ ★

IÁLYSOS

With its wide bay lapped by an azure sea, mild winters, cool summers, water sports, modern hotels and vibrant nightlife, Iálysos is a popular holiday destination.

Ancient Iálysos lay on the northwest slopes of **Mt Filérimos**. A road signposted from Triánda winds its way up to the summit that was once the acropolis. Here lie the most interesting remains: a 13th-century monastery, the foundations of the classical temple of Athena Polias and traces of Phoenician paving.

The **Church of our Lady of Filérimos** is the most impressive building on the mountain. From the outside it looks like a single structure, yet it includes no less than four chapels and a monastery (restored during Italian occupation). In the innermost of the chapels is a mosaic floor with the early Christian symbol of the fish.

To the left of the stone stairway leading up to the church is the entrance to a subterranean Byzantine chapel – **Ayios Georgios** – decorated with frescoes by the Knights of St John during the 14th and 15th centuries.

A 4th-century Doric water fountain was exposed on the southern side of Mt Filérimos during a landslip in 1926. Refreshment of a different kind is now sold on Mt Filérimos, namely Sette Herbe (seven herbs), a delicious liqueur made from a recipe devised by Italian monks.

The Cross of Filérimos
A gigantic cement cross, erected by the Italians, can be visited on Mt Filérimos if you are keen to make the short detour along a tree-lined path. The cross, lit up at night, is visible from very far away. Unless you are claustrophobic you may enjoy climbing up to the cross arms. Be careful, however, as the staircase is very tight and allows for one-way traffic only! The view from the top is splendid.

16

IÁLYSOS & PETALOÚDES

See Map D ★ ★ ★

PETALOÚDES

Petaloúdes, Valley of the Butterflies, is well signposted. From Faliráki or Afándou on the east coast make for Psinthós and follow the signs for Petaloúdes from the village square for 7km (4 miles).

In summer, coaches bring visitors to this spot. They are led down through the cool tree-filled valley to see shady rocks and tree branches covered with thousands of moths – not butterflies. The display is created by a single species: **Jersey tiger moths** (*Panaxia quadripunctaria*) gather in the valley during July and August in great numbers, attracted by secretions of resin from the bark of the liquidamber trees. The moths show their chocolate-and-white forewings when they are settled and at rest; when disturbed they reveal brilliant orange underwings that are spotted with black.

Petaloúdes is a pleasant place for nature **walks**. It has good paths, several waterfalls and lengths of wooden bridges. In the brief Rhodes autumn another spectacle takes place when the leaves of the liquidamber turn bright orange-red before falling.

Most visitors have no time to explore, but there is a pleasant one-hour walk to **Panayía Kalópetra** (Moní Kalópetra), built by Alexander Ypsilántis in 1782. The path to the monastery leads uphill through the Valley of the Butterflies.

Don't Disturb
The outstanding feature of Petaloúdes is its myriad moths, and countless tourists come to photograph them. While at rest the striking patterns of the moths' wings are not visible and this tempts many ignorant visitors to clap or shout in order to disturb the resting insects. Then they take their unforgettable snapshot of a flurry of moths desperately attempting to regain a cool, shady spot, and leave.

Anyone headed for Petaloúdes should know, however, that the diurnal resting period is vital in the moths' reproductive cycle and, thus, for future generations of flying jewels. Sadly, their numbers have dwindled alarmingly as a result of human intrusion into their secret valley.

Below: *Moní Kalópetra, en route to Petaloúdes.*

HIGHLIGHTS

Ancient Kámiros
🕐 Tue–Sun: 08:00–
19:00 in summer;
09:00–15:00 in winter.
Closed on Mondays.
✉ 30km (19 miles)
west of Rhodes Town.
💻 www.rodos.com/
kamiros
💰 4 Euros.
🚌 Buses leave from
Rhodes Town and stop
along the coastal road, a
short walk (about 1km)
from the historic site.

◎ See Map C	★ ★ ★

ANCIENT KÁMIROS

Archaeological evidence suggests that a Minoan settlement existed here. Rebuilt as a Hellenistic city after a violent earthquake in 226 BC, it was abandoned after another one in AD 142 and covered by dust and earth. Thus no-one looted the settlement for stone and its layout has remained intact.

The site entrance leads on to the lower or temple terrace – with remains of a large supporting wall at its northern boundary. Little of the Doric temple remains but on the terrace's east side is a row of sacrificial altars, the largest dedicated to Helios, the island's patron. In the residential area of the ancient town are remains of **baths**, a **well-house**, some larger **houses** with portions of columns and parts of the **drainage system**. The enormous cistern further up supplied the town with water. The crowning feature of ancient Kámiros was a 3rd-century-BC **stoa** comprising two rows of Doric columns that ran for some 200m (656ft) along the ridge above the town.

Below: *The calm vista from the stoa of Ancient Kámiros.*

ANCIENT KÁMIROS & MONÓLITHOS

See Map E–C3   ★ ★ ★

Below: *View of the Crusader castle Kastrou Monólithos.*

MONÓLITHOS

Mt Akramítis (823m; 2700ft) falls to the sea at Monólithos, which forms the southwestern end of Rhodes' mountainous spine.

A lonely, spectacular Crusader castle, **Kastrou Monólithos**, stands impregnable at the top of an enormous rock pinnacle,

Monópetros (meaning 'single rock'), about 240m (787ft) high. From some angles the castle looks truly inaccessible – and this was certainly the original intention – but today steps lead up to it from a car park below, allowing visitors to ascend the summit.

Of the castle, only the walls, which were built by Grand Master Pierre d'Aubusson (1500), remain – together with the whitewashed church of **Ayios Panteleímon**.

The views from here are simply staggering and, understandably, the castle is one of the top tourist attractions on Rhodes island. Numerous coaches visit daily to deposit eager sightseers armed with cameras and binoculars. The visitor numbers fall dramatically towards the end of the day, however, and it is then – in the warm glow of the late afternoon and early evening – that the castle looks at its best and most romantic.

Monólithos village lies just off the main road. It has remained quite untouched by the pressure of modern tourism.

Above: *The scarlet turban buttercup grows around Cape Prasonísi in spring.*

✿ See Map E–A5	★★★

CAPE PRASONÍSI

Cape Prasonísi, which literally translated means 'green island', forms the southernmost tip of the island of Rhodes. The headland is separated from the coast, joined only by a narrow sandy isthmus.

The swell on the Aegean side of the spit to the west makes it a windsurfers' paradise, and in summer large numbers of enthusiasts make their way here in hired jeeps along the rough road from Katavía. Several *tavernas* provide ample sustenance and many visitors camp here (unofficially). On the eastern side of the headland the sea is generally much calmer although in rough winter seas the isthmus disappears altogether.

In springtime Cape Prasonísi is an unbelievably idyllic place, remote and undisturbed, where it is possible to be the only one on the spectacular sandy beach.

This is also the time when the surrounding countryside begins to shrug off winter and bursts with birdsong and an amazing variety of wildflowers – wild **anemones**, the striking **scarlet turban buttercup** (*Ranunculus asiaticus*) and beautiful **orchids** are to be seen.

Just a few weeks later the scrub explodes into flower with colourful bushes of rockroses providing bold patches of shimmering white or pink blooms, and sometimes beneath them, growing on the roots, you may find the yellow and red parasitic plant cytinus (*Cytinus hypocistus*).

Cape Prasonísi

🚌 Bus leaves from Rhodes Town at around 14:30 on Tue, Thu and Sat bound for Mesanagros, Lahania and Kattavia. It leaves from those towns between 07:00–08:00 on the same days – bound for Rhodes.

The bus leaves Rhodes Town at around 14:30 on Mon, Wed and Fri bound for Apolakiá, Profilia and Istrios. It leaves from those towns between 07:00–08:00 on the same days – bound for Rhodes.

The best way to get around is by hired vehicle, but don't be tempted to leave the road – this area is a militarized zone.

CAPE PRASONÍSI & LÍNDOS

See Map A, B	★ ★ ★

LÍNDOS

Only 56km (35 miles) from the capital on good coastal roads, Líndos is a spellbinding destination. Canny visitors take a boat excursion and are rewarded with superb views of the lovely bay and – the village's crowning glory – its ancient acropolis. Clinging to the slopes below are the dazzling **Captains' Houses**, built in the 16th and 17th centuries by – as the name suggests – merchant seafarers.

Líndos' **acropolis**, later fortified by the Knights of St John, now forms part of the ruins within massive walls that are accessible on foot or by donkey-ride. The **Bay of St Paul** below the acropolis is where the apostle is said to have landed during a storm in AD 51.

Líndos is reputed to be one of the hottest places on the island, both in temperature and as a measure of its nightlife. The town beach offers safe swimming in crystal clear water. Popular with families, it can become very crowded. **Péfki**, 5km (3 miles) south of Líndos, is a good alternative, with a sandy beach and excellent water sports.

Tourist Information
✉ Main Square, Líndos
☎ (0244) 31-428, or 31-227.

Plateia Eleftherias
🕐 08:00–21:00 daily.

Pallas Travel
Try them for accommodation.
☎ (0244) 31-494,
📠 (0244) 31-595.

Líndos Sun Tours
Car and motorcycle hire.
☎ (0244) 31-333,
🖥 www.lindianet.gr

Below: *Charming Líndos, a National Historic Landmark.*

⚙ See Map E–F5   ★ ★ ★

**Arhángelos'
Specialities**
Traditional Greek carpets
may be bought at
Arhángelos. They are
woven on smaller looms
than Turkish carpets,
but are just as beautiful,
although of coarser
texture. Popular designs
are dolphin, bird and
deer motifs set inside
a geometric pattern.
    Also available are
handmade leather boots
and attractive ceramics.

ARHÁNGELOS

This large and prosperous village is situated
7km (4 miles) south of Kolímbia. Surrounded
by citrus groves, it is famous for its **fruit production** and **village crafts** – pottery, footwear
and hand-woven carpets are made here. Its
name comes from the village churches of
the Archangel Michael and the Archangel
Gabriel – the former has the distinctive tiered
bell tower (the 'wedding cake' campanile)
found in the islands of the Dodecanese.

Many traditional aspects of village life are
preserved in Arhángelos, from Rhodian village houses with brightly painted doors and
walls, to local speech which preserves an old
dialect and traditional songs. In the narrow
streets of the old quarter of the village you
can wander around and see the traditional
'above-knee-high' boots being made. These
hide boots once offered villagers essential
protection against snakes; they now make a
popular but pricey souvenir.

Below: *Villagers of
Arhángelos main-
tain proud traditions
in crafts, song and
in local dialect.*

Arhángelos castle was built in 1467 on
the order of Grand Master Orsini. It is now

little more than a set
of massive walls, but
once served as one
of 12 fortresses that
had been built to
protect the coasts
from pirate raids.
Today, the site pro-
vides excellent views
over the village, with
its bell tower and
green citrus groves,
and to the sea.

See Map G–A2 ★★★

Below: *One of the cool forest streams at Eptá Pigés.*

EPTÁ PIGÉS

The name Eptá Pigés, 'seven springs', refers to the streams that feed a small artificial lake and a waterfall built by the Italians, who dammed the valley 4km (2.5 miles) inland from Kolímbia.

In the dry summer months, the verdant Eptá Pigés becomes one of the most popular tourist spots – an oasis of greenery.

There is a pleasant **woodland walk** to the site from the turn-off signposted for Eptá Pigés, or you can drive to the café in the woods. The lake is reached by a path over the hill or a pedestrian tunnel beneath it. The tunnel is 186m (610ft) long, and quite damp and dark and thus a passage only for those who do not suffer from claustrophobia.

There are peacocks in the valley, but naturalists know that a greater attraction is the number of rare, **wild orchids** that grow locally. The scrubby hills just after the turning for Eptá Pigés are filled with strange orchids that imitate insects in shape, colour or scent to attract them for pollination. Note **King Ferdinand's orchid** (*Ophrys regis-ferdinandii*) and the **pink butterfly orchids** (*Orchis papilionacea*). And keep an eye out for **Violet Limodore** (*Limodorum abortivum*) which grows among the pine needles in the valley.

> **Wild Orchids**
> Some species of wild orchids, like the genus: *ophrys*, mimic insects in shape, colour and scent in order to attract them for pollination. On Rhodes there are **late spider orchids** (*Ophrys fuciflora*), tiny blue-bottle-like flowers of **King Ferdinand's orchid** (*Ophrys regis-ferdinandii*) and **Reinhold's orchid** (*Ophrys reinholdii*), a bee orchid with pink sepals and deep brown lip patterned with white. Other orchids include the pink **naked man** (*Orchis italica*) and tall spikes of the **violet limodore** (*Limodorum abortiyum*). Rhodes boasts over 40 orchid species.

⚓ See Map G–C4 　　★ ★ ★

Above: *Tsambíka Bay viewed from Mt Tsambíka.*

TSAMBÍKA BAY

On the coastal road just to the south of Kolímbia, lies sweeping Tsambíka Bay. Good for swimming and with breathtaking views, it is understandably popular with visitors, especially during the main holiday season (from July to August).

Mt Tsambíka (326m; 1070ft), rises above the bay and is the location of a celebrated monastery – a tiny **Byzantine church** that is dedicated to the Virgin Mary and contains an 11th-century icon. If determination and modern medicine have failed to produce a pregnancy, then a pilgrimage to **Tsambíka Monastery** on September 8 to pray to the Virgin Mary is said to be able to produce the desired result. Local lore claims that children whose birth was aided in this way were named in honour of the monastery: Tsambíka for girls and Tsambíkos for boys (indeed, very common Rhodian names).

The small monastery can be reached on foot along a steep path that climbs up from the car park below. At the top, visitors can catch their breath, get their cameras ready and drink in the views. Arguably, this walk rewards visitors with the very finest vista on the entire island. The superb panorama stretches down to the nearby coast, with Tsambíka Bay framed by a gentle, azure sea.

Distance from Rhodes Town: 25km (15 miles)

🚌 Buses leave from Rhodes Town at 09:00 and return from Tsambíka at 16:00.

See Map E–H4 ★★★

FALIRÁKI

Faliráki rivals Ixiá as the most popular package resort on Rhodes and with good reason – there is so much to do here. The 5km (3-mile) beach with its grey sands is gently shelving, and has earned the coveted Blue Flag awarded for excellence. Amenities (umbrellas, showers and cabins) are excellent and **water sports** enthusiasts can enjoy a range of activities. The 'longest water slide in Greece' is located in the gardens of the Hotel Pelágos. At the far, less crowded end of the bay is the island's only official nudist beach.

Away from the beaches, mini-golf, go-karting and bungee-jumping are available, and the resort even boasts its own aquarium-cum-vivarium, the **Faliráki Snake House**.

The **shopping mall** at Faliráki Bay North, where many of the expensive hotels are located, is one of the best on the island.

After dark, the incessant disco music is a reminder that Faliráki has a special appeal for the 18–30 set, though there are enough bars, restaurants and nightclubs to satisfy most tastes and age groups.

The Water Park
Faliráki's Water Park offers something for fun lovers of all ages. There are 'Thrill Rides', 'Multi Rides', 'Taking it easy rides' and 'kids only rides', as well as unique splash pools and water slides.
☎ (02410) 84-400
🕐 Low season: 09:30–18:00; peak season: 09:30–19:00.
🖥 www.water-park.gr
✆ info@water-park.gr
🚌 The park's free bus operates daily, every hour, from Mandraki harbour. There is also a boat from Rodos town and Faliráki center. A free shuttle runs to and from the park for guests staying at one of the six Esperia hotels in Faliráki.
🍴 There is a wide selection of food and beverages available within the park.

Below: *Faliráki, one of Rhodes' popular holiday playgrounds.*

Kastellos

A ruined Crusader fortress sits impressively on a rocky outcrop overlooking **Kámiros Skála** some 130m (427ft) below. Known locally as **Kastellos** (but signposted **Kástro Kritinías**), it was begun by the Knights of St John in 1309; the tower and walls were added later. Its superb strategic position enabled the Knights of St John to command some 75km (47 miles) of coast.

Below: *The harbour at Kámiros Skála – good for fresh fish and the Chálki ferry.*

KÁMIROS SKÁLA

This delightful fishing harbour some 16km (10 miles) south of ancient Kámiros is often cited as the port from which the ancient town once exported its fine ceramics. Recent excavations, however, contradict this claim.

Kámiros Skála now has the distinction of being the only functioning **fishing port** on the west coast of Rhodes – its three *tavernas* serve the freshest fish, a fact well known to organized coach parties which make a lunchtime stop there. Otherwise, the place is remarkably peaceful. The harbour is also the departure point for ferries to the island of Chálki (*see* page 71), which connect with the bus service between Rhodes Town and Kritinía or Monólithos. The ferry acts as a 'lifeline' for the inhabitants of Chálki who shop and sell their wares in Rhodes and send their children to school there. There is a ruined **Christian basilica** in the village and on a rock wall near the port you can see a Hellenistic gravestone with an unfinished, rather worn relief.

See Map E–D3

★ ★

Below: *Kritinía village nestles at the foot of Mt Atáviros.*

KRITINÍA

It is well worth making a detour into Kritinía, just a few kilometres further along the main road from Kámiros Skála.

The cluster of sparkling, white-washed houses clinging to the mountain slope lend this settlement a unique charm. The tiny village church in Kritinía, **Ayios Ioánnis Prodhrómos**, dates from the late 12th century and its frescoes span the 13th–15th centuries. The village square looks out over the coast and there are two pleasant *tavernas* in which to sit and relax; a **folk museum** lies just outside the village on the main coast road to Rhodes Town.

The road beyond Kritinía offers breath-taking scenery with the bulk of Mt Atáviros always on the left and the land falling steeply to the sea on the right. The horizon is broken by small islands which seem to become more hazy as the day warms. At times, perspective creates the effect of an entire chain of islands stretching out from the coast – **Makrí**, **Strongíli**, **Tragoússa** and **Alimniá** towards **Chálki**. There is a pleasant boat trip that runs daily in summer from Kámiros Skála via the group of islands to Chálki and back again, giving the visitor enough time to stop and explore Chálki.

Kritinía or Crete
The first settlers in this part of the world are said to have been Minoans who named the place after their island homeland *Kriti* (**Crete**).
Althaimenes, grand-son of King Minos of Crete, is the reputed founder of Kámiros and Kritinía. Apparently, when he became homesick he used to climb Mt Atáviros because it is said that you can see all the way to Crete from the summit on a clear day.

Below: *Retsina, a resinated wine, is an acquired taste.*

 See Map E–D3

EMBÓNAS

This prosperous little village in a depopulated region is dedicated to weaving and to the production of wines. Another very lucrative industry is the 'Greek evening' to which tour operators bring their eager clients in droves.

The choice elevation, land aspect and soil types of the surrounding region create certain microclimates that are ideal for viticulture of several varieties of grapes. The **Emery wine factory** in Embónas is open to visitors and affords the chance to taste its products. If the factory is too crowded then Embónas also has more than its fair share of *tavernas* which serve local wines.

On the other side of the mountain lies **Ayios Isídoros**, another very picturesque village set in tiers on the southeast slopes of **Mt Atáviros**. A clear path zig-zags its way up to the summit (a tough climb, especially in hot weather); the energetic can carry on down the other side to Embónas (approximately six hours in all). A right turning from the road north out of the village takes one onto the poorly surfaced track towards **Laérma**, 11km (7 miles) away, which claims to be at the very centre of the island. Typical of an inland village, the pace here is slow, and the villagers mostly elderly.

The Emery Wine Factory
🕐 07:30–15:30 Mon–Sat; coach parties between 10:00–14:00 on request.
✉ Situated on the northern side of the village.
☎ (0246) 41-208.
📧 triantaf@hol.gr
💻 www.emery.gr
🍷 Free tastings every weekday.
🚌 Hotels in Embónas can advise on half- and full-day excursions.

See Map E–B4 | ★★

APOLÁKIA

Apolákia is the largest village in the far south, an agricultural settlement famed for its watermelons. The *tavernas* and rooms for rent make the village a good base for walkers, especially since Apolákia is well served by buses and no car is needed.

The gravel track from Apolákia to **Siána** (11km; 7 miles) can be walked comfortably in about three hours. Approximately 4km (2½ miles) north of Apolákia it runs past a large **reservoir** where the valley has been flooded. The church of **Ayios Theotókou** is to the right just before this reservoir, and the tiny church of **Ayios Theoros** lies a few hundred metres beyond. The **Monastery of Ayios Georgios o Vardos**, some 3km (2 miles) walk from Apolákia on a track branching off from the road to the dam, has some superb frescoes. A road running west to east connects Apolákia with **Gennádi** on the opposite coast. Short detours bring you into hill villages – Arníthea, Istríos, Profilía and Vatío – with their tranquil pace of life.

Village Homes

Many of the mountain villages still have distinctive one-roomed houses with a corner fire place and few (if any) windows.

These traditional village houses, though several hundred years old, follow a much earlier pattern dating back to Crusader times. Their simplicity stems from inheritance laws which meant having to provide for daughters.

Following her marriage, the eldest daughter would be given the house and contents as a dowry. The poor father was also obliged to provide houses for any other daughters and the solution was to build basic, functional homes of one room.

Below: *The reservoir near Apolákia is a favourite area for walkers and hikers.*

See Map E–D5 ★ ★

God of Healing
Asklepios, god of healing, was son of the god **Apollo** and the mortal woman, **Coronis**. His success as a physician was legendary: he was killed by an angry **Zeus** for bringing a patient back from the dead and was then revived as an immortal. Followers of the god in the ancient world had a dual role as priest-physicians – an Asklepeión was a temple where they ministered to the sick.
Hippocrates, father of medicine, was the most famous of the Asklepiadae.

Below: *The best bread on Rhodes is baked at Asklipío village.*

ASKLIPÍO

Asklipío lies directly inland from Kiotári and is reputed to be the birthplace of the Greek god of healing – **Asklepios** (Aesculapius), the son of Apollo. In ancient times the village was a centre of healing to which islanders would have made pilgrimages and where the followers of Asklepios exerted a dual function as priests and healers of the sick. A ruined castle dominates the village, but most visitors come to see its superb church, the Monastery of Metamórfossi, or **Kimísis Theotókou**, a domed 11th-century Byzantine basilica with 15th-century frescoes depicting scenes from the Old Testament. Next to the church is a small **village museum** set up by the villagers. Bread is still made in the early morning in communal wood-fired ovens (*foúrnos*) – there is no food in the Hellenic world to compare with warm village bread.

See Map E–F5   ★ ★

FÉRAKLOS

Below: *A ruined citadel broods above Féraklos.*

The **ruined citadel** above Féraklos is an imposing sight, especially from a distance: it was once one of the best fortified strongholds of the Knights of St John. Before they arrived on Rhodes in 1309, the island had been overrun by Muslim pirates who occupied the original Byzantine structure. The Knights expelled the marauders, improved the fortifications and used it as prison. In this fortress they were able to resist Süleyman and held out under siege for some time after Rhodes Town fell.

There is little to see at the fortress except walls and bushes, but the views of **Haráki Bay** to the south and **Agáthi beach** to the north are superb, making the climb well worthwhile. A track leads from Féraklos castle to Agáthi beach. Though relatively short on facilities, it boasts superb golden sands and is good for swimming. Development for a hotel complex is underway and across the beach there is the diminutive church of **Ayia Agáthi**, built into a cave.

> **Lines of Defence**
> The Knights set up a defensive chain on Rhodes: the seven major castles are at **Kritinía, Arhángelos, Asklipío, Féraklos, Líndos, Monólithos** and **Rhodes town**. Many watchtowers (*pyrgos*) were also built.
> Castles were constructed on neighbouring islands as a system of outer defences: **Chálki, Kálimnos, Kos, Tílos, Léros, Níssyros** and **Sými**. The Knights brought in skilled craftsmen from southern Europe schooled in the latest architectural and engineering techniques, and their piratical acts introduced a supply of slave labour.

See Map E–F4   ★ ★

Above: *14th-century frescoes inside Ayios Nikólaos Fountoukli.*

ELEOÚSA

Many people visit **Profítis Ilías** by travelling up from the west coast (Soroni) or from the east coast (Kolímbia) to the village of Eleoúsa and then taking the road further up to the summit. The 15th-century Byzantine chapel of **Panayía Eleoúsa** just on the edge of Eleoúsa has some lovely frescoes dating from the 17th and 18th centuries. The remains of an Italian-built plaza form the square of the charming little village.

About 3km (2 miles) from Eleoúsa on the minor road leading to the summit is the pretty church of **Ayios Nikólaos Fountoukli** (St Nicholas of the Hazelnut), famous for its 14th-century frescoes and a dome which sits on a stone drum. It originally formed part of a late Byzantine monastery and inscriptions inside show it was dedicated to the memory of three children.

Near the summit of Mt Profítis Ilías there is a small settlement, as well as the large twin chalets, **Elafos and Elafina** (Stag and Doe), of a mountain hotel – closed at the time of writing. A path laid out by the Italians leads from a small chapel dedicated to Elijah (Ilías) around the summit ridge. The summit itself is a military outpost and out of bounds to visitors.

Spring Water
The friendly village of Sálakos, 3km (1.9 miles) north of Mt Profítis Ilías, is home of Nymfí, the locally produced spring water. If it is a truly Greek village atmosphere you're after, why not book into **Sálakos' Hotel Nymfí**, ☎ (0241) 22-206.

☼ See Map E–H4   ★ ★

KOSKINOÚ

On a steep rise just inland from Ayia Marína lies the charming village of Koskinoú which, in Ottoman times was inhabited only by Turks. Asgouroú, a suburb of Rhodes on the road to Koskinoú, still has a small Moslem population and a mosque (once the Church of Ayios Ioánnis).

Koskinoú is one of the prettiest villages in Rhodes and a good place to see Rhodian houses dating from the 17th and 18th centuries. The houses have brightly painted doors and their flower-filled courtyards are paved in the traditional way with black and white pebbles (*hochláki*).

A road from the village leads to the coast, 2.5km (1.6 miles) away, where there are hotels and *tavernas*, as well as the springs at **Thermes Kalithéas**, recommended by Hippocrates for their power to relieve arthritis. When the Italians restored this spa in the 1920s they built a distinctly Moorish pavilion with pink marble pillars and surrounded it with lush gardens. Its former splendour has faded, but the spa still attracts visitors.

Thermes Kalithéas has a small beach, served by a regular bus service from Rhodes, but it can get very crowded.

> **Koskinoú Traditional House**
> ⏱ Open daily 09:00–13:00 and 18:00–20:00; Sat 10:00–13:00; closed on Sun.

Below: *Houses in quaint Koskinoú have gaily painted windows and doors.*

Above: *Today's Süleyman Mosque occupies the site of an earlier one built in 1523 by Süleyman the Magnificent.*

Places of Worship

Basilica Church of Ayios Fanoúrios, Rhodes Town

Just off Platía Ariónos, hidden by old houses, lies this church whose Byzantine frescoes grace an unusual barrel vault.

⊠ *Platía Ariónos, Old Town.*

Süleyman Mosque, Rhodes Town

Sultan Süleyman the Magnificent built the original mosque in 1523 to mark his conquest of the island. Today's impressive pink structure, surmounted by a dome, was built in 1828. It is open for prayers only and not to the general public. Following Ottoman invasion, churches in Rhodes Town and in the main towns of other islands were converted into mosques. Bell towers were restructured to become minarets, while any human or animal image found on the inside was hidden under white paint, in keeping with Islamic principle. Statues were removed and carved tombstones set into church floors were covered with carpets.

⊠ *Sokrátous St, Turkish Quarter;* ⊕ *Not open to the public.*

Moní Skiádi

An icon of the Virgin Mary is kept in the 13th-century chapel of this monastery. At Easter it is carried in procession down to the coast and from there to the island of Chálki (*see page 27*).

A *panayíri* (festival) is held every year on 8 September to celebrate the birthday of the Blessed Virgin. ⊠ *4km (2½ miles) west of Messanagrós.*

Moní Thári

This monastery, dedicated to Archangel Michael, was completed in the 13th century using parts of an earlier church. ⊠ *Located southwest of Laérma.* ☉ *Can be viewed if someone is there to let you in.*

Church of the Assumption of Our Lady, Líndos

Just off the central square of Líndos, this church was built in the 14th century and restored in 1490 by Grand Master Pierre d'Aubusson. There was further restoration under Italian occupation in 1927. The late Byzantine frescoes (painted by Gregory of Sými) date from around 1779. One of them depicts St Francis of Assisi with

a donkey's head – a fine example of pagan irreverence found in Byzantine paintings. The church floor is a black-and-white pebble mosaic (*hochláki*). ⊠ *Main Square.*

Ayios Georgios Chostos, Líndos

Some frescoes in this, the oldest church on the island, date from the iconoclastic era (8th–9th century AD). ⊠ *Plaça Santa María.*

Saints' Days

Apart from Easter, village *panayíris* are held in honour of the saint to whom the village church is dedicated. In Kremastí festivities last a week, beginning on the eve of the saint's day. The day itself starts with a church service and street parade. Peripheral events make it one of the biggest festivals in Rhodes, if not in the Dodecanese.

Below: *The bell tower of Ayios Georgios Chostos.*

Below: *The Inn of Auvergne in the Collachium.*

Historic Buildings

The Collachium, Rhodes Town

All buildings associated with the Knights' order were housed in the Collachium, including their living quarters. Begin your exploration just inside the **Liberty Gate** at **Platía Simis** (Arsenal Square) – here are the remains of a 3rd-century temple of Aphrodite, as well as a useful large map of the town. Other classical remains have been excavated behind the Ionian and Popular Bank. Many of the Knights' buildings are clustered near **Platía Eleftherías** and the adjacent square, **Platía Argirokástrou**. The **Inn of Auvergne** stands on the east of the square – above the portal is the coat of arms of Guy de Blanchfort, the Grand Master who completed the elegant building in 1507 (recently renovated).

✉ *Old Town of Rhodes.*

The Street of the Knights, Rhodes Town

Ippotón, Street of the Knights, follows an ancient road that led from the harbour to the Temple of Helios where the Knights built the Palace of the Grand Masters. On the right of it lie, in order: the **Inn of Italy** (built by Fabrizio del Caretto in 1519), the **Inn of France** (1492, Emery d'Amboise), **Zizim House** (named after Sultan Beyazit's brother, who was given asylum there), the **French Chapel** and the **Inn of Provence**. The **Inn of Spain** is on the left side of the street. Today, the buildings house various institutes and galleries and most have lovely courtyard gardens.

The Palace of the Grand Masters, Rhodes Town

The Palace of the Grand Masters is said to be a reconstruction of a palace built by Helion de Villeneuve on the site of an ancient temple to the sun god, Helios. The Turks at one time used it as a prison, for stabling horses and as a gunpowder store. It was destroyed by the **Great Gunpowder Explosion** of 1856, when lightning struck a minaret, exploding the magazine inside. The Italians reconstructed it as a summer home for Victor Emmanuel III (later used by Mussolini). The renovation, completed in 1939, is not to everyone's taste. Although architects ensured fidelity in the outer features, the interior owes little to the Knights and much to Italianate design.

The Roman and Early Christian floor mosaics from Kos are superb examples of mosaic art. ☎ *(0241) 23-359,* ⊕ *Tue–Sun 08:30–15:00.*

The Captains' Houses, Líndos

Built by merchant seafarers in the 16th and 17th centuries, these charming houses have doorways decorated with cables and other nautical motifs. Pop into a courtyard and you'll see lovely ceramic plates (originally the souvenirs of voyages) hanging on the walls.
Tourist Information, ⊠ *Platia Eleftherias,* ☎ *(0241) 31-900,* ☏ *(0241) 31-288.*

Above: *The Palace of the Grand Masters dominates the skyline of Rhodes Town.*

> **Wall to Wall**
> The Knights replaced much of the Byzantine town walls but kept the old foundations. They employed the construction skills of Italian engineers and the labour of numerous slaves. Each 'Inn' had responsibility for a section of the walls and construction went in phases according to the enthusiasm and ambitions of the reigning Grand Master.
> The walls stretch for some 4km (3 miles) with ramparts and turrets, and have an average thickness of 12m (39ft). A moat 30m (98ft) wide protected the landward side.

Above: *Sun god Helios, patron of Rhodes (190 BC).*
Opposite: *There is no record of what was sacrificed on this altar at Kámiros.*

Colossus of Rhodes

A sculptor from Líndos, Chares, was in charge of the construction of the Colossus, a figure that took 12 years to finish and stood over 30m (98ft) high. Legend has it that it straddled Rhodes harbour.

One of the **Seven Wonders of the Ancient World**, it was toppled into the harbour in 225BC by a violent earthquake and lay corroding until AD653 when the Saracens sold it as scrap. Accounts note that it took 900 camels to carry away the bronze to waiting cargo vessels.

Museums and Galleries

Museum of Decorative Arts, Rhodes

Situated in the south wing of the former Knights' Hospital, the Museum of Decorative Arts houses needlework, Rhodian wall plates, costumes, tools and furniture, as well as complete rooms of old houses displaying folk art from the Dodecanese.

✉ *Old Hospital of the Knights (Palazzo dell' Armeria), Old Town,* ☎ *(0241) 21-954,* ⏰ *Tue–Sun 08:30–15:00.*

Archaeological Museum of Rhodes

Construction of this former hospital began in 1440 under Grand Master Jean Bonpart de Lastic whose crest, supported by two angels, stands above the entrance. The Infirmary Hall is now a display area for heraldic devices of the Crusaders – tomb carvings and their coats of arms. The classical collection spans the Mycenaean to late Hellenistic periods, with many objects that were discovered in tombs at Iálysos and Kámiros (*see pages 16 and 39*).

The best known items in the museum are two statues of the goddess Aphrodite. The kneeling Small Aphrodite (90BC) shows the goddess combing her hair. Venus Pudica or Modest Aphrodite dates from the third century BC and was recovered from the seabed by fishermen in 1929. Other treasures include a head of Helios (150BC), and the famous grave stelae found at Kámiros.

✉ *Museum Square, Old Town,* ☎ *(0241) 27-657,* ⏰ *Tue–Fri 08:00–19:00, Sat/Sun 08:00–15:30.*

The Byzantine Museum, Rhodes Town

The 11th-century church of Panayía tou

Kastrou (Virgin of the Castle) houses a collection of Byzantine paintings and icons.
✉ *Ippotón Street,* ☻ *Tue–Sun 08:30–15:00.*

Rhodes Jewish Museum

This museum, situated in rooms at the Kahal Shalom synagogue, documents and preserves the unique history of Rhodes' Jewish community.
✉ *Dosiadou Street;* ☻ *daily 10:00–16:00 (April to November).*

Ottoman Library

Opposite Süleyman Mosque (*see* page 34), this library was founded in 1794 by Ahmed Hasuf. It houses several Persian and Arabic documents as well as some fine handwritten old Korans.
☻ *09:00–16:00, Mon–Sat,* 💰 *Free.*

Fun For Children
Aquarium of Rhodes

Built to international standards, this interesting subterranean aquarium comprises some 40 display tanks filled with sea creatures including turtles.
✉ *Kos Street, Rhodes New Town,*
☎ *(0241) 27-308,*
📠 *(0241) 78-321,*
🖥 *hsr@rhs.rho. forthnet.gr* ☻ *Apr–Oct 09:00–21:00, Nov–Mar 09:00–16:30.*

The Water Park

Children love the water park at Faliráki (*see* page 25).

Culture Vultures

Rhodes, along with Alexandria, became a centre of learning and culture to rival Athens in the third century BC. Rhodian sculptors like **Chares of Líndos** and **Pythocritus** attracted pupils and followers from all over Greece.

Although the cultural explosion associated with classical Greek civilization was centred on Athens, the islands also produced notable figures: Hippocrates (Kos), Pythagoras (Sámos) and Sappho (Lésbos).

Discovery

Ancient **Kámiros** was rediscovered in 1859 when villagers uncovered a few graves. The British Consul at the time and French archaeologist Saltzmann then began excavating and discovered rich tombs. As so often happened at the time, many of the finds ended up outside Greece in Britain, Paris and Berlin. As new tombs are found in the hills around Kámiros their exciting finds (stelae and ceramic ware) are now housed in the **Archaeological Museum of Rhodes**.

Below: *A view from the Municipal Gardens to the Palace of the Grand Masters.*

Parks and Gardens
Municipal Gardens, Rhodes

Cypress trees and tall palms offer welcome shade in summer and make the Gardens a pleasant place for a stroll. The Gardens are also the site of a spectacular *Son et Lumière* (sound and light show) every evening that recounts the thrilling tale of the Knights, including their fall during the siege of Süleyman.
⊠ *Alexandrou Papagou St, ⊕ 20:15, English performances most nights. Greek, French, German and Swedish shows also held.*

Rodíni Park

The Knights once grew medicinal herbs in Rodíni Park, which is today a favourite with native Rhodians and visitors alike. It is attractively set out with trees, a rose garden and bridges spanning small lakes. In late August it hosts the Rhodes Wine Festival but in ancient times it rang to different sounds – Aeschines established his School of Rhetoric here in 342BC (see page 7).
⊠ *3km (1.9 miles) from Rhodes Town, along road to Líndos. Buses leave terminal at New Market every half hour.*

ACTIVITIES
Sport and Recreation

For Greek men in particular, the one thing that ignites national passion more than political happenings is **football**. When national or international matches are being played at the large stadium in Rhodes Town, the atmosphere is unforgettable.

But for many visitors Rhodes' major attraction is the incredibly wide range of **water sports** that is on offer at all of the larger resorts on the island. Yachtsmen and windsurfers especially will be thrilled by the near-perfect conditions along the island's west coast. Families with children have the choice of a number of safe, sheltered bays where a warm sea laps golden beaches, providing hours of fun in the sun.

Budding naturalists and the more serious botanists and ornithologists will delight in the island's floral splendour and rich birdlife. Seasonal shows of wildflowers and orchids draw admirers from far and wide, while the annual spring and autumn migrations to and from the breeding grounds in northern Europe are sure to delight birdwatchers.

Before you Dive in

If you prefer under-water sport, rather than splashing about on the surface, be aware of the following points:

• Scuba divers need to be in possession of the relevant international diving qualifications.

• Dive only where you are allowed to do so and ensure that the difficulty of the dive is in tandem with your level of experience. If you are a novice, in need of a refresher course or going to attempt a difficult dive, rather hire an experienced local dive guide to come along with you. (See page 43.)

• Respect the local rules and regulations and do not damage or destroy marine life or archaeological remains.

Below: *Líndos Beach is the epitome of an ideal seaside holiday.*

Above: *Ideal conditions have made windsurfing an enjoyable sport on Rhodes.*

In and on Water

For visitors who have come to Rhodes in search of summer fun centred on the beach, the west coast is ideal.

For the active there are pedaloes, yachts, motor boats and jet skis for hire. And for the not-so-active there are comfortable sunbeds and umbrellas – essential, not only for shade, but as wind breaks when the *meltémi* (*see* page 6) gets a little too fresh.

On the west coast there is almost a constant breeze – much more of a benefit than inconvenience in the baking summer temperatures. Beach showers placed at frequent intervals allow you to wash off the salt after cooling in the sea.

The persistent breeze is strong enough to create a good swell and to fill the sails of yachts and windsurfers. Suitably experienced windsurfers will make for Cape Prasonísi (*see* page 20) and the westward side of its sandy isthmus for some of the best windsurfing on Rhodes, and then back up the coast around Apolákia Bay. East coast resorts also offer windsurfing.

Beginners need not feel left out as many of the larger hotels and holiday complexes along the resort strip from Ixiá to Triánda (*see* page 15) offer equipment and tuition. Boards are also available for hire from a few independent outlets.

IN AND ON WATER

For details of windsurfing schools in Rhodes, contact the **Greek Windsurfing Association in Athens**, ☎ (01) 323-3696.

Divers and snorkellers will want to venture under the waves as soon as possible, where they will discover sea urchins and a wide variety of colourful fish such as peacock wrasses and scarlet soldier fish. Even the occasional octopus can be spotted around the rocky coastal areas.

Divers should note that scuba diving is very carefully controlled because of the chance of finding valuable antique artefacts that can be spirited out of the country (as has happened in the past).

In Rhodes, diving is only permitted through two centres that also offer courses from beginners to advanced: **Waterhoppers Diving School**, ☎ (0241) 38-146, and **DMC** (Dive Med Centre), ☎ (0241) 61-115. Both are well established and qualified. The DMC also organizes wreck searches and sea-bed surveys.

Along the Shore
Rhodian beaches are not rich in shells. Little is washed up because the tidal rise and fall is so small. Occasionally after winter storms, however, beachcombers find brownish, hairy balls formed from sand and the broken leaves of a marine plant, **Neptune grass** (*Posidonia oceanica*).

Below: *Popular but not crowded – the sand and shingle beach at Kolímbia.*

43

Knights of St John
In 1070 a group of
Italian merchants in
Amalfi founded a reli-
gious and charitable
order of Benedictine
Knights – the Knights
of St John. The order's
first patron saint was
St John the Almsgiver
of Cyprus. Members
became known as the
Knights Hospitallers
through their role in
protecting pilgrims and
caring for the sick.
Originally there were
some 600 Knights
drawn from noble
families and ruled by a
Grand Master. They
were divided into eight
'inns' on the basis of
'tongues' – Auvergne,
France, Provence, Italy
Germany, England and
the division of Spain
into Aragon and Castile.

Walking Tours
Along the Walls and Gates of Rhodes

The walls and gates to the Old Town are
the legacy of the Knights Hospitallers of St
John who bought the island in AD1306 and
took possession three years later.

Work on the construction of the citadel
was completed in 1346 and was inspired by
the papal palace in Avignon, France. The
Knights lived within a walled enclosure
known as the Collachium (see page 36).
Although the Hospitallers was a semi-
monastic order they became extremely
wealthy, benefiting in particular from the
dissolution (in 1312) of their rivals, the
Knights Templar.

Sources differ over the number of gate-
ways – originally each section of wall had its
own entrance, but during the Ottoman
period the two facing the harbour were
blocked up. **Liberty Gate** (Píli Eleftherías)
dates only from 1924 and was built to
permit traffic access. Points of entry to the
Old Town are at Liberty Gate at the northern
corner just off Mandráki harbour and, anti-
clockwise, at: **d'Amboise Gate**, **St George's
Gate**, **St Athanasius Gate**, **Koskinoú (Ayios
Ioánnis) Gate**, **St Catherine's Gate**, **Thalassíni
Gate** and back to the **Arsenal Gate** just east
of Liberty Gate.

Below: *The massive
towers of Thalassíni
(Marine) Gate.*

You can walk the 4km
(2.5 miles) around the
walls on the outside at
any time – access to the
walls themselves is only
via a guided tour.

The walk begins at
the massively fortified
d'Amboise Gate which

was built in 1512 by Grand Master Emery d'Amboise (1505–12). A bridge spans the multiple ditch outside and deer graze in the moat. The German Knights held the wall from here to St George's Gate, next to which is a bas relief depicting St George killing the dragon. Beneath it is set the coat of arms of Antoine Fluvion,

who was Grand Master from 1421–37.

The Knights of Auvergne defended the stretch as far as the Tower of Spain (1489) – this, like many other parts of the wall, was constructed during Pierre d'Aubusson's industrious tenure. The section of wall from the Tower of Spain to St Athanasius Gate was defended by Spanish Knights. It was here that Süleyman entered before sealing off the gate (re-opened by the Italians).

The next section as far as Koskinoú Gate was guarded by English Knights, while Knights of Provence kept the following section as far as the Tower of Italy or Del Caretto Tower (Fabrizio del Caretto was Grand Master from 1513–21) and Italian Knights, were entrusted with the walls up to St Catherine's Gate. The Knights of Castile protected the long section of wall overlooking the harbour as far the Arsenal Gate. The massive and solid Thalassiní (Marine) Gate, approximately half way along the stretch, has three impressive towers.

Above: *Three of an original 13 medieval windmills remains at Mandráki harbour.*

What's in a Name?
Rhodos literally means Rose Island and yet, roses as one usually thinks of them do not grow on Rhodes. The roses in question could however be the pink and white rock roses which appear in spring. Greeks sometimes use words as generic terms, so the term rose may have been a general one making Rhodes the 'Island of flowers'. The name could also have come from 'roidon' (a local word for pomegranate) or from the Phoenician word for snake 'erod', a reference to the serpents on Rhodes in ancient times?

Above: *The slopes of Mt Profítis Ilías offer good walks.*

Around Monólithos

Situated between Monólithos and its castle, Kastrou Monólithos, is a track that leads north towards the coast at **Pyrgos** where there is a **medieval watch-tower** (*pyrgos*). It forms part of a warning system that included the castle situated between Kámiros Skála and Kritinía.

The road is negotiable by vehicle and after about 3km (2 miles) it divides. To the left is a detour to Pyrgos and to the right lies a mountain road skirting Mt Akramítis. Take the left detour on foot.

Around Eleoúsa

There is another superb walk east from Ayios Nikólaos Fountoukli (which lies 3km; 2miles from Eleoúsa on a minor road that leads up to the summit of Mt Profítis Ilías). It winds through the mountain forests to **Sálakos**. Just before the track reaches the main road into Sálakos there is an old cobble track (*kalderími*) along which donkeys carried provisions to the top of the mountain via a series of 'switchback' bends. There is now a very popular walk on paths initially laid out by the Italians. The track skirts a military barracks on the summit itself.

The quaint village of Sálakos makes a very good base for walkers interested in longer stays and more thorough exploration of the area. It boasts a few *tavernas*, as well

---

Around Monólithos
Location: Map E–C3
Distance: 3km
(1.9 miles)
Duration: 50 minutes
Start: Monólithos
Finish: Monólithos
Route: Affords magnificent views of the surrounding forest and mountains.

Around Eleoúsa
Location: Map E–F4
Distance: 12km
(7 miles)
Duration: Allow 4 hours
Start: Sálakos
Finish: Eleoúsa
Route: Pass through the most beautiful woods in Rhodes.

WALKING TOURS

as a *pension*. Also of interest is the little 14th-century chapel of **Kimisis Theotokou** which has a beautiful pebble mosaic floor.

The Butterfly Walk

The dramatic walk from Moní Kalópetra (*see* page 17) to Petaloúdes, Valley of the Butterflies, follows a river valley – the return route is along the higher, wider track. From this latter track another runs uphill to the south and then curves westwards on a forest road to **Ayios Soulas Monastery**. The chapel of **Ayios Geórgios**, just above Ayios Soulas, is reached after about three hours of walking along ridges with breathtaking views to the coast.

Around Stégna

The coastal paths running north and south from Stégna are marked by bright red dots painted on rocks. The path north to **Tsambíka Bay** runs along the coast and then swings inland and up and over a rocky ridge. The view of Tsambíka Bay from the top is electrifying and the descent to the bay takes you down an enormous dune slope. It is impossible to resist the temptation to swim here and, when cool, contemplate the ascent of Mt Tsambíka at the far end of the beach.

For the route south – Stégna to Agáthi and Haráki – allow around 1½–2 hours, following the clifftops past Mt Profítis Ilías. Views towards Féraklos castle and all the little bays before it are truly breathtaking.

Around Stégna
Location: Map E–F5
Distance: 12km (7 miles)
Duration: 4 hours
Route: Crosses a landscape of rock formations and beautiful bays.

Below: *Meadows filled with flowers await walkers in March and April.*

Beekeepers
Beekeepers make good use of the scrubby hill-sides around Siána. In spring and summer especially, the country-side is full of nectar-rich flowering herbs and trees. The locally produced **honey** is on sale in the village. Mixed with **yoghurt** and eaten with locally baked **bread** it makes an excellent breakfast.

Birds and Butterflies

In spring and autumn large numbers of birds visit the island en route to and from their breeding grounds in northern Europe.

Martins, swifts and swallows are some of the first to arrive: wheatears, pipits and larks (including the shore lark) appear in fields. Raptors, such as honey buzzards, harriers and red footed falcons, can be seen soaring high on thermals. Lesser kestrels breed on Rhodes with colonies near Líndos; peregrine falcons can occasionally be spotted along rocky coasts near Monólithos.

The most colourful arrivals are the **rollers** with their metallic-blue plumage and dipping flight, and **bee eaters** which appear in large numbers in the south of the island towards Cape Prasonísi.

Around Monólithos, Kámiros Skála and Mt Atáviros there are **blue rock thrushes**, **crag martins**, **ravens** and even, occasionally, **alpine swifts** and **peregrine falcons**.

From April onwards **butterflies** appear. Most obvious are **swallowtails**, and a swallowtail relative, the **festoon**. In mountain glades you will find the **Cleopatra**: lemon-yellow with orange patches. **Hawkmoths** are common, especially the tiny **hummingbird hawk** that flies by day and will drink from the edge of a glass. The attractive **Jersey tiger moths** can be seen at Petaloúdes (*see* page 17), while **great peacock moths** look like small bats as they cruise around the mercury vapour lamps in Rhodes Town.

Below: *The southern festoon (Zerynthia polyzena), a spring butterfly species.*

ENTERTAINMENT
Nightlife

Butterflies of a different kind emerge at night when Rhodes Town becomes a magnet for hedonists. Bars, clubs and no-frills *tavernas*, especially in the New Town, do a roaring trade and disco-goers can party until dawn in sophisticated establishments like **Le Palais** or **Amazon**. Music is everywhere – from traditional Greek (try **Elli Beach** for its Bouzoúki Club) to themes for aged rockers (**1960 Bar** in Diakou Street or **Sticky Fingers Pub** in the New Town). For formal Greek dance, **Nelly Dimoglou Theatre** (Andronikou Gardens, off Platía Arionos) offers performances by its world-renowned company. And if a wave of nostalgia should overcome visitors with Emerald Isle connections, there is Irish music and Guinness at **Flanagan's** in Orfanidou Street, Old Town.

Faliráki has quite a few night spots (*see page 25*) that offer everything from cool dance vibes provided by imported DJs to karaoke, and satellite television coverage of international soccer and boxing events.

Above: Tavernas *in Hippocrates Square, Rhodes Old Town, are popular, especially when the sun goes down.*

Gay and Lesbian Travellers

There is no law against homosexuality and several of the Dodecanese islands, especially Rhodes and Kos, have become popular with gay travellers. Bear in mind, however, that the strict Greek Orthodox church does not condone homosexuality and thus, neither will many Rhodians. It is best to respect the local viewpoint and avoid public displays of affection. For information on gay bars in Rhodes Town try:
⌨ www.geocities.com/WestHollywood/2225/ or ⌨ www.jwpublishing.com/comguidegreece.html

business, and can be confusing sometimes, even to Greeks.
For essentials it is best to try between 08:30 and 13:30. If a shop does open for the afternoon it will be about 16:30–20:00. In the resorts, shops stay open all day until around 22:00.

Resort and Hotel Gift Shops

In almost every hotel, and certainly in the tourist resorts, visitors will discover the typical souvenir shop. Items range from tacky mass-produced goods to beautiful examples of traditional crafts such as carved olive wood and jewellery.

Museum Shop of the Ministry of Culture

Sold here are remarkably good reproductions of classical jewellery and castings of statues and friezes. ⊠ *Near the Museum of Decorative Arts, Old Hospital of the Knights, Old Town.*

Shops

Rhodes Town has everything from modern shopping malls to designer boutiques and the bustling former Turkish Bazaar in the Old Town. Most of the small shops on the island cater almost exclusively for the tourist market. Items for sale range from handmade traditional ware to jewellery, food and drink. The opening hours vary according to the nature of the

Bookshops

Booksellers are quite rare on Rhodes so it is advisable to stock up either at home before you depart or in Athens on your way in. In the UK, **Hellenic Book Service** stocks a large selection of new and used books about Greece in both Greek and English. Contact them at ⊠ 91 Fortress Road, Kentish Town, London NW5 1AG, ☎ (020) 7267-9466.
Newspapers and international magazines reach the islands the following day. The *International Herald Tribune* includes an English version of *Kathimerini*, the Greek daily newspaper.

Arhángelos Pottery and Carpet Shops

Arhángelos, where you can watch the artisans at work, is the place to buy pottery and hand-woven rugs. All of the souvenirs here have a truly Rhodian flavour. The distinctive colours and natural themes (flowers, birds and fish) of the pottery are attributed to an Eastern influence. The Knights, so it would appear, indulged in a little piracy and captured a Persian merchant ship complete with craftsmen. The Rhodians are said to have learned their trade from them.

Shops in Líndos

Lace and embroidery work are ancient Líndian traditions – items are displayed on the rocks that lead up to the acropolis and in shops in the village. Brightly painted Líndian plates and other pottery items are favourites with visitors.

Also look out for leather goods, such as thonged sandals, belts, wallets and handbags.

Inland Shops

The little shops found in mountain villages sell olive wood carvings and ceramics, as well as finely embroidered linen, beautiful hand-woven carpets and delicate lace. Also, be sure to sample the wonderful local produce ranging from honey and olive oil to such delicacies as bottled olives, nuts, capers, and tempting cakes and pastries.

Wine Shops

The range of Emery wines is on sale and available for tasting at the winery in Embónas (see page 28).

Music Shops

If it is authentic Greek music you are after, both traditional and more recent pop tunes, try and steer away from souvenir shops and the occasional market stalls.

(see page 28).

What to Buy

Hidden among the numerous repositories of souvenir tat on Sokrátous Street, are shops selling the wares of craftsmen – leather goods, gold jewellery, sandals, rugs, table linen, ceramics, sponges and umbrellas with every designer logo you can imagine. It is worth haggling a bit if paying cash.

The Ministry of Culture operates a museum shop near the Museum of Decorative Arts selling remarkably good reproductions of classical jewellery and castings of statues and friezes.

Opposite:
Distinctive Rhodian plates, geared to the souvenir trade, are sold at many shops and markets.
Below: *In villages such as Arhángelos, ladies can be seen weaving and selling traditional carpets.*

Below: *Interesting souvenirs can be bought at market stalls in the streets of the Old Town.*

Manual Music Centre
Have a great selection of Greek music.
✉ *25 Martiou Street 10,* ☎ *(0241) 28-266.*

Jewellery Shops
Many rich visitors descend on the jewellery shops in Rhodes as part of their luxury cruise stopovers. Although gold jewellery, in general, is competitively priced, it is still rarely affordable for the ordinary tourist. If it is good quality gold you're after, however, Rhodes is where to buy it.

Rodos Gold Vogiatzis
One of the world's largest jewellery exhibitions displays an exclusive collection of high quality jewellery. It also houses a museum of jewellery, as well as the largest goldsmith workshop in the Agean where visitors may watch craftsmen at work.
✉ *Rhodes – Lindos Avenue (near Faliráki),* ☎ *(0241) 08-6040,* ✆ *(0241) 08-6121,* ✆ *rod-gold@ mail.otenet.gr* ⌨ *www.rhodos-info. de/rodosgold*

Gregory Katsaridis Exclusive Jewellery Workshop
Here you will find a selection of shiny, dull or hammered.gold jewellery inspired by Classical, Hellenistic, Byzantine and Modern art. Also have a variety of precious stones.
✉ *83 Ermou Street, Rhodes Old Town,* ☎ *(0241) 07-8670,* ✆ *(0241) 03-0355,* ⌨ *www.rhodos-info. de/gregory*

Left: *Sokrátous Street, the busiest thoroughfare in the Old Turkish Quarter.*

Markets
The Bazaar

On Sokrátous Street in the Old Town, hidden among repositories of souvenir tat, are shops that sell the wares of true craftsmen. Here you will find leather goods, jewellery, sandals, rugs, table linen, ceramics, sponges and umbrellas with every designer logo you can imagine. There are some bargains to be found and it is worth haggling a bit over the price, particularly if you're paying cash.

⊠ *Sokrátous Street, Old Town.*

The New Market

Many shops around the New Market periphery are excellent for locally produced wines and spirits, dried nuts and olives. Fresh fruit and vegetables are piled high at stalls in the courtyard, which has the fish market at its centre. Stalls selling fresh *tiropittes* (cheese pastries), pizza or *souvlákia*, make picnic lunches a very tempting prospect indeed. Look out for Emery's Villaré, a prize-winning dry white wine that is reckoned to be among the best in Greece.

⊠ *Mandráki harbour.*

The Sponge Industry

The industry which made the sponge divers of Chálki and Kálimnos wealthy was hit by 'sponge blight' which decimated the creatures in the early 20th century. Now most sponges for sale on the islands come from the coasts of Sicily and North Africa.

In early times divers descended into the depths on a lifeline weighed down by stones. Later, the invention of diving equipment led to problems as divers suffered from nitrogen narcosis (the bends) from diving too often and resurfacing too quickly.

Above: *The modern Esperos Palace Hotel in Faliráki.*

Domatía

An ever-popular option with budget travellers, *domatía* offer a bed-room, usually without meals. Most are open from April to October, and promoted by touts from June to August.

An ABC-rating system determines the price you are quoted. Another determining factor is whether bath-room facilities are private or shared.

In the past, spare rooms were let out to summer visitors. These days many *domatía* are purpose-built, often with their own facilities (including kitchenette), adjoining the main house. As a rule they are scrupulously clean and comfortable.

If you arrive out of season, try to negotiate the price in your favour.

WHERE TO STAY

From June to early September most island hotels are geared to the prebooked pack-age trade – look for last-minute bargains from your local travel agents.

Out of season it is easy to find a room – prices are 30% lower than in high season. Prices are government controlled according to category (Deluxe, AA, A, B, C, D and E). By law, these rates have to be displayed in each hotel room.

Many smaller hotels close out of season but people are often glad to rent rooms and are open to gentle bargaining. **Tourist Information** (EOT) and the **Tourist Police** on Rhodes have lists of rooms for rent. The **NTOG** in Athens (*see* page 85) has informa-tion on accommodation (including *pen-sions*) on Rhodes and the other islands. Local people go to the harbour to meet fer-ries and offer rooms for rent. Greek ladies are house-proud and the accommodation will be simple but spotless.

There are no **youth hostels** on Rhodes and there is only one **campsite**. It is near Faliráki and is open from April to October, ☎ (0241) 85-515 or 85-516 or 85-358.

Rhodes Town

(Map F)

In this town, advance booking is advisable as (in season) independent accommodation is impossible to find. The island is a year-round resort and popular for winter breaks. Out of season, accommodation is more readily available.

• LUXURY
Grand Hotel Rhodos (Map F–B2)

An immense swimming pool, tennis courts, a nightclub and the only casino on the island. Breakfast is included in the price.
- ⊠ 1 Akti Miaoúli,
- ☎ (0241) 26-284,
- 🖶 (0241) 35-589,
- ✆ grandhotel@ ellada.net
- 🖳 www.ellada. net/mitsis

Rodos Park Hotel
(Map F–B5)

Completed in 1995, this is a comfortable, well-appointed hotel that overlooks the Municipal Gardens.
- ⊠ 12 Riga Fereou,
- ☎ (0241) 89-700,
- 🖶 (0241) 24-613.
- ✆ info@rodospark.gr
- 🖳 www.rodospark.gr

• MID-RANGE
Hotel So Nikol
(Map F–D6)

Comfortable rooms in a superb old house. Rooftop terrace has views over Old Town.
- ⊠ 61 Ippodhámou,
- ☎ (0241) 34-561.

Spartalis (Map F–D3)

Comfortable and friendly, with a pleasant breakfast terrace; situated opposite the quay, useful for connecting ferries.
- ⊠ Odhos N Plastíra,
- ☎ (0241) 20-406,
- ✆ info@ spartalis-hotel.com
- 🖳 www.spartalis-hotel. com/eng

Victoria (Map F–D3)

A friendly family-run hotel close to Mandráki harbour.
- ⊠ Odhos 25 Martíou,
- ☎ (0241) 24-626.

Cava d'Oro
(Map F–F5)

A beautifully restored 15th-century house with an inner courtyard; close to the commercial harbour. All rooms have a shower and a toilet.
- ⊠ 15 Odhos Kisthiniou, Old Town,
- ☎ (0241) 36-980,
- 🖶 (0241) 77-332,
- ✆ hotel@cavadoro.com
- 🖳 www.cavadoro.com

• BUDGET
Hotel Paris
(Map F–D6)

Located in the Turkish Quarter. Clean, friendly with a courtyard surrounded by citrus trees.
- ⊠ 88 Ayios Fanoúriou,
- ☎ (0241) 26-354.

Iliana Hotel
(Map F–F6)

Delightful old house in Jewish Quarter with terrace and bar.
- ⊠ 1 Gavála,
- ☎ (0241) 30-251.

Pension Andreas
(Map F–D6)

Basic, clean, friendly; delightful courtyard, views over the Old Town and coast.
- ⊠ 28d Odhos Omirou,
- ☎ (0241) 34-156,

✆ (0241) 74-285,
📠 andreasch@
otenet.gr

Hotel Hermes

(Map F–D4)

Ideal for island hop-
pers. Luggage can be
left by arrangement.
✉ 7 Nik. Plastira St,
near Mandráki Quay,
☎ (0241) 26-022,
✆ (0241) 33-160.

New Village Inn

(Map F–C2)

Comfortable, nicely
furnished, in a quiet
street; single and
double rooms.
✉ Kanstantopedos 10,
☎ / ✆ (0241) 34-937,
📠 newvillageinn@
rho.forthnet.gr

Western Resorts

In season it is imposs-
ible to find accommoda-
tion on the west coast
so book in advance.
There are many studios
and self-catering apart-
ments for hire. In win-
ter, resorts are unlikely
to be very full – at this
time some hotels cater
for the international
conference trade.

Paradíssi has apart-
ments but aircraft
noise can be a prob-
lem. Useful for a bed
when arriving late or
leaving early from
the airport.

• LUXURY

Armonia Apartments

(Map E–H3)

Beautifully furnished
apartments within
easy reach of the
seafront.
✉ Kremastí,
☎ (0241) 29-420.

Filérimos Hotel

(Map E–H3)

Fine rooms, apartments
and a good taverna.
Has two swimming
pools; 10 minutes'
walk to the beach.
✉ Triánda,
☎ (0241) 92-510.

Grecotel Rodos Imperial (Map E–H3)

Generally regarded as
the island's top hotel.
Everyone (including
children) and every-
thing is catered for.
Sports, restaurants,
Greek language and
dancing lessons.

✉ Leoforos Ialissou,
Ixiá, ☎ (0241) 75-000,
✆ (0241) 76-690,
🖥 www.grecotel.gr

Hotel Sunflower

Map E–H3

Small hotel with good
facilities. Caters for
international clientele.
✉ Triánda,
☎ (0241) 93-893,
✆ (0241) 94-270.

Rodos Palace

(Map E–H3)

Well-equipped high-
rise hotel with its own
indoor and outdoor
pools, gym, sauna and
tennis courts. Apart-
ments and bungalows;
even a royal suite.
✉ Trianton Avenue,
Ixiá Bay,
☎ (0241) 25-222,
✆ (0241) 25-350,
📠 info@rodos-palace.gr
🖥 www.rodos-palace.gr

Mira Mare Wonder-
land (Map E–H3)

Bungalows in mature
gardens on lovely long
beach. Perfect for
family holidays.
✉ Ixiá Beach,
☎ (0241) 96-251,
✆ (0241) 95-954,

🕏 info-miramare@
mamhotel.gr
🖳 www.mamhotel.
gr/miramare

**Cosmopolitan
Hotel** (Map E–H3)
Positioned across the
road from the beach.
Large pool and good
facilities for children.
✉ Iraklidon Street,
Ixiá Bay,
☎ (0241) 25-281,
📞 (0241) 32-823.

• **MID-RANGE**
Solemar (Map E–H3)
Large hotel close to
the beach; 10 minutes
by bus from Rhodes
Town. There is a
restaurant and
swimming pool.
✉ Sotiros Street 66,
Ixiá, ☎ (0241) 96-941,
📞 (0241) 90-212.

Leto (Map E–H3)
Beachfront hotel in a
smart resort.
✉ Ixiá,
☎ (0241) 23-511,
📞 (0241) 20-310,
🕏 litohtl@otenet.gr

**Sunflower
Illiotropio** (Map E–H3)
Friendly 74-room hotel.

✉ Just off main west
coast road, Kremastí,
☎ (0241) 93-893.

Sabina (Map E–G3)
Friendly, efficiently run
hotel with 70 rooms.
✉ Theológos Beach
(Thólos),
☎ (0241) 41-613,
📞 (0241) 41-681,
🕏 sabina@rodhotel.gr
🖳 www.rodhotel.gr/
sabina

Hotel Meliton
(Map E–G3)
Well-appointed with
swimming pool and
tennis courts.
✉ Theológos Beach
(Thólos),
☎ (0241) 41-666.

• **BUDGET**
Artemis (Map E–D2)
Modest, clean pension
with seven rooms.
Friendly owners – very
good value for money.
✉ Kámiros Skála.

Thomas Hotel
(Map E–C3)
Small, friendly hotel –
each room has a kit-
chenette and fridge.
✉ Monólithos,
☎ (0241) 22-741.

Afándou
• **LUXURY**
Afándou Beach
(Map E–G5)
Largest hotel in
Afándou with 90 beds.
Near the mixed sand
and shingle beach.
✉ Afándou,
☎ (0241) 51-586.

Lydia Maris
(Map E–G5)
The swimming pool is
the central feature of
this holiday complex.
✉ Kolímbia,
☎ (0241) 56-294/41,
📞 (0241) 56-424.

Xenia (Map E–G5)
Situated on an 18-hole
golf course and offers
three separate swim-
ming pools for cooling
off after the game.
☎ (0241) 51-121.

Arhángelos
• **MID-RANGE**
Karyatides
(Map E–F5)
A small, well-appointed
hotel about 1km
(0.6 miles) from the
town centre; has a
swimming pool and bar
selling Greek snacks.
☎ (0244) 22-965.

Anthi Sun

(Map E–F5)
Comfortable, modern
hotel in large, well-
maintained gardens.
☎ *(0244) 22-619.*

Stégna

Antonis (Map E–F5)
Friendly family-run
pension of seven
apartments, close to
the beach.
☎ *(0244) 22-280.*

Faliráki
• *LUXURY*
Esperos Village

(Map E–H4)
Self-contained com-
plex that dominates
Faliráki beach. Three
swimming pools and
well-equipped chil-
dren's playground.
✉ *6.5km (4 miles)
northeast of Faliráki,*
☎ *(0241) 86-046,*
📠 *(0241) 85-741,*
🖥 *www.helios.gr/
hotels/esperos-village*

**Faliráki Beach
Hotel** (Map E–H4)
In its own grounds
fronting the beach.
The restaurant has its
own *taverna.* Close
to town.

✉ *Faliráki Beach,*
☎ *(0241) 85-301,*
📠 *(0241) 85-675,*
🖥 *www.rodos.com/
faliraki-bch*

Hotel Rodos Beach

(Map E–H4)
Hotel and bungalows.
The beach, with water-
skiing and windsurfing,
is a short walk through
the hotel gardens.
✉ *Kalithéas Bay, 5km
(3 miles) northeast of
Faliráki,*
☎ *(0241) 85-412.*

• *MID-RANGE*
**Cannon Bar
Pension** (Map E–H4)
Friendly, clean and
affordable rooms.
✉ *Poseidon Street,*
☎ *(0241) 85-596.*

• *BUDGET*
Hotel Dimitra
(Map E–H4)
In town, a comfortable
family-run hotel, open
March to December.
Good value.
☎ *(0241) 85-309.*

Kalithéa
• *LUXURY*
Castello di Rodi
(Map E–H4)

Well situated for
access to thermal
baths (2km; 1 mile),
with own sauna,
gardens and pool.
✉ *Kalithéa,*
☎ *(0241) 64-856,*
📠 *(0241) 64-812,*
🖋 *info@
castellodirodi.gr*
🖥 *www.
castellodirodi.gr*

• *MID-RANGE*
Kalithéa (Map E–H4)
A small, clean hotel
with 15 rooms.
☎ *(0241) 62-498.*

Kolímbia
**Kolímbia Beach
Hotel** (Map E–G5)
Friendly, comfortable
hotel of modest size.
✉ *Kolímbia,*
☎ *(0241) 56-247,*
📠 *(0241) 56-203,*
🖋 *kolymbia-beach@
rho.forthnet.gr*

Koskinoú
Paradise
(Map E–H4)
Luxury hotel on the
bay; water sports,
restaurants and a
night club.
☎ *(0241) 66-060,*
📠 *(0241) 66-066.*

WHERE TO STAY

Líndos

Because Líndos is a National Heritage Site no new hotels may be built. Village houses converted for holiday use are often linked to specialist operators. To rent village houses:

Direct Greece
✉ Granite House, 31 Stockwell Street, Glasgow G1 4RY, ☎ London (020) 8785-4000, ✆ (020) 8785-1515.

• LUXURY
Líndos Sun
(Map E–E6)
Small hotel and bungalow complex.
☎ (0244) 31-458.

Líndos Mare
(Map E–E5)
Near old Líndos town, modern four-star hotel built above Vlícha Bay.
✉ Vlícha Beach, ☎ (0244) 31-130, ✆ (0244) 31-131, 🖥 www.helios.gr/hotels/lindos-mare

• BUDGET
Fedra Rooms
(Map E–E6)
A selection of bed-rooms available, with bathrooms.
✉ Opposite Church of Agia Panazia, ☎ (0244) 31-286.

Gennádi

• LUXURY
Lydian Village
(Map E–D5)
Tastefully designed and furnished complex built around courtyards.
✉ Between Lárdos and Gennádi, ☎ (0244) 44-161, ✆ (0244) 44-165.

• MID-RANGE
Dennis (Map E–C5)
Quiet, nicely furnished, clean apartments.
✉ Gennádi Beach, ☎ (0244) 43-395, 🖥 www.rodos.com/lindos/dennis

Effie's Dream Apartments
(Map E–C5)
Quiet location with beautiful views.
✉ At the northern end of the village, ☎ (0244) 43-410, ✆ (0244) 43-437, 🖎 dreams@srh.forthnet.gr

Panorama Gennádi
(Map E–C5)
Small, family-run hotel, close to sea.
☎ (0244) 43-315.

Betty Apartments
(Map E–C5)
Good, furnished apartments, accommodates twelve.
☎ (0244) 43-020.

Kaláthos
Atrium Palace Resort (Map E–E5)
Resort hotel with huge swimming pool, children's pool, bars, sun terraces as well as a beach.
✉ Kaláthos Beach, ☎ (0244) 31-601, ✆ (0244) 31-600, 🖎 atrium@otenet.gr 🖥 www.atrium.gr

Lárdos Bay
• LUXURY
Rodos Princess
(Map E–D5)
Situated close to the beach 5km (3 miles) north of Gennádi.
✉ Kiotári, ☎ (0244) 47-102, ✆ (0244) 47-267, 🖎 info@rodos-princess.gr

ACCOMMODATION

- *MID-RANGE*
Kiotári Beach
(Map E–D5)
Small self-contained hotel with sea views.
✉ *Asklipio, Lárdos Bay,*
☎ *(0244) 43-251.*

Hotel Elioula
(Map E–D5)
Small hotel (36 rooms), 300m from beach; swimming and paddling pools, snack bars and a TV lounge.
✉ *Lárdos Beach,*
☎/📠 *(0244) 44-594/5,*
🖥 *www.rodosnet.gr/ Elioula*

- *BUDGET*
Fedra (Map E–D5)
A friendly family-run hotel in the centre of the village.
☎ *(0244) 44-218.*

Péfkos
Summer Memories
(Map E–E6)
A small and friendly establishment with just 14 beds.
☎ *(0244) 41-500.*

Vlícha Bay
- *LUXURY*
Steps of Líndos
(Map E–E5)

Quiet hotel with pool and facilities for water sports in the bay. It occupies a commanding position on a hillside overlooking the bay. The beach is a 10-minute walk downhill.
☎ *(0244) 31-062,*
📠 *(0244) 42-267.*

Neighbouring Islands
Most accommodation is prebooked during peak season. On all islands tourist police have lists of rooms for rent. Ask for directions – some places do not provide street addresses or numbers. Locals often meet boats or ferries and offer rooms for rent.

Chálki (Emborío)
- *LUXURY*
The Captain's House (Map E–B1)
A delightful mansion with a sophisticated atmosphere (three rooms only). Book well in advance.
✉ *On the northern side of the harbour,*
☎ *(0246) 45-201.*

- *MID-RANGE*
Hotel Chálki
(Map E–B1)
Fairly unusual accommodation in the former sponge factory. The only hotel on Chálki and very comfortable.
☎ *(0246) 45-208,*
📠 *(0246) 45-208.*

Nick's Taverne
(Map E–B1)
Self-contained rooms; they serve very good food in the *taverna*.
✉ *Póndamos beach,*
☎ *(0246) 57-248.*

Níssyros
- *MID-RANGE*
Miramare Apartments
(Map H–C2)
Comfortable apartments with lovely sea views.
✉ *Near Palia,*
☎ *(0242) 31-100,*
📠 *(0242) 31-254.*

- *BUDGET*
Xenon Hotel
(Map H–C2)
Cheerful, cheap; handy for the ferry.
✉ *Mandráki harbour,*
☎ *(0242) 31-011.*

Sými (Yialos)

• *LUXURY*
The Dorian
(Map H–E2)
Lovingly restored
Captain's House. Quite
expensive but superb.
☎ (0241) 71-181.

Hotel Aliki
(Map H–E2)
Beautifully restored
Captain's House with
antique-furnished
rooms.
☎ (0241) 71-665.

• *MID-RANGE*
Hotel Metapontis
(Map H–E2)
Attractively painted in
traditional fashion;
pricey but charming.
☎ (0241) 71-077.

Tílos (Livadía)

• *LUXURY*
**Olympus
Apartments**
(Map H–C3)
Self-contained, well-
appointed apartments
with views.
✉ Above Livadía,
☎ (0246) 44-365.

• *MID-RANGE*
Marina Rooms
(Map H–C3)

A friendly hotel;
rooms with balconies
and great views over
the gulf and village.
☎ (0246) 44-066,
📠 (0246) 44-169.

• *BUDGET*
Pension Anna
(Map H–C3)
Friendly and very clean.
✉ Just outside Livadía.
☎ (0246) 44-357.

Kárpathos

• *LUXURY*
Possirama Hotel
(Map H–C6)
Well-equipped self-
catering apartments
with own balconies.
Open April–October.
✉ Affoti beach,
Pigádia,
☎ (0245) 22-251,
📠 (0245) 22-929.

Pension Romantica
(Map H–C6)
Pension in its own
citrus orchard – can
accommodate 28.
☎ (0245) 22-460/1.

• *MID-RANGE*
Chryssiakti Hotel
(Map H–C6)
Friendly and comfort-
able, good restaurant.

✉ Diafáni, near quay,
☎ (0245) 51-215.

Kos

• *LUXURY*
**Hippocrates Palace
Hotel** (Map H–C1)
Expensive spa hotel.
✉ Kos Town,
☎ (0242) 24-401,
📠 (0242) 24-410.

• *MID-RANGE*
Afendoulis
(Map H–C1)
Friendly quiet *pension.*
✉ 1 Evripilou,
☎ (0242) 25-321.

• *BUDGET*
Pension Alexis
(Map H–C1)
A favourite with
younger travellers.
Owner speaks English.
✉ 9 Irodotou,
☎ (0242) 28-798,
📠 (0242) 28-797.

Kos Camping
(Map H–C1)
Well-equipped camp-
ing site reached by
minibus from the
ferry. Has its own
shop, taverna, kitchen
and laundry.
✉ Eastern Waterfront,
☎ (0242) 23-910.

Rhodian Fast Food
Fast-food outlets and international restaurants with menus in English, German and Swedish are well established in Rhodes. *Oúzeria*, though mainly drinking establishments, also serve snacks (*mezédhes*). **Street stands** (*girós*) serve sandwiches (*híro*) and kebabs (*souvlákia*) to take away or eat at a table. **Estiatórias** are essentially restaurants, usually more upmarket than *tavernas*. **Psáro-tavernas** specialize in fish, and **Psistarías** sell spit-roast meats.

Below: *Delicious* mezédhes *(starters) are almost a meal in themselves.*

EATING OUT
Food and Drink

Greek food bears favourable comparison with any Mediterranean cuisine. Watch to see where the locals eat, rather than rush to an obvious tourist establishment. In cosmopolitan Rhodes, most restaurants have learned that other Europeans like their food hot – not tepid ('better for the digestion'), as is the Greek custom.

Mezédhes (Starters)

Greek starters are a lavish affair – an appetizing invitation to tuck in and explore a variety of new tastes. Don't rush it; take time to savour the following: *taramasaláta* (made with smoked cod's roe), *tzatzíki* (yoghurt with garlic, mint and cucumber), *eliés* (green or black olives), *rossikisaláta* (potato salad with mayonnaise), *yigándes* (haricot beans in tomato sauce or vinaigrette), *kolokithákia* (deep-fried courgette) served with *skordhália* (a simple garlic sauce), *mavromatiká* (black-eyed beans), *sagnáki* (fried cheese), and small pasties of cheese (*tiropitta*) or spinach (*spanachópitta*).

Vegetarian Food

Many of the eating establishments cater well for vegetarians. The idea of not eating any meat through choice is accepted, but in fact remains totally alien to Greeks. In Greek a vegetarian is called *hortofágos* (grass eater) – which says it all. Local fruit and vegetables are excellent in season.

Fish and Meat

Fish tends to be expensive in Rhodes and is usually imported these days. (Local catches have shrunk due to over-fishing.) Worth trying are: *barboúnia* (grilled red mullet), *marídhes* (fried whitebait) and *xifia* (grilled swordfish marinated in oil and lemon). *Kalamarákia* (deep-fried squid) is excellent, especially when it is fresh. *Garídhes* (shrimps or prawns) are delicious, but invariably expensive.

Some of the tasty meat dishes that you will find on menus are *keftédhes* (meatballs), *biftékia* (a sort of rissole-cum-hamburger), *souvlákia* (grilled kebabs), *arni psitó* (roast lamb) and *katsíki* (roast kid).

Pastries

Rhodians have a sweet tooth and prefer buying their cakes and pastries from a *zacharoplastía* (patisserie-cum-café) rather than ordering them at a restaurant. Some of the pastries are very sweet and sticky. *Baklavá* is nut-filled puff pastry soaked in sugar syrup and *kataifi* is chopped walnuts and honey wrapped in shredded wheat. Both are delicious.

Honey, usually of the very runny kind, is a favourite in Rhodes, often served over creamy fresh yoghurt. Useful lunchtime or picnic stand-by's are the larger versions of the pasties mentioned on page 62 made with filo pastry: *tiropitta* (minted cheese filling), *spanachópitta* (spinach and cheese) or *elíopitta* (filled with black olives).

Above: *Tasty fast food, Greek-style, is available from kebab sellers.*

Above: *Though only a small part of its economy, wine production on Rhodes is growing rapidly.*

Wine

In antiquity, Rhodes had a reputation for its excellent wines – thus viticulture is a proud tradition on the island that goes back 2400 years.

Modern methods of production have recently been introduced and are yielding wines that are well worth trying. Most vines are grown inland from the cooler west coast, around Embónas (*see* page 28).

There are two main producers in Rhodes. KAIR, a cooperative started in 1924 by the Italians, has a new plant at Koskinoú (*see* page 33) and an old one in Rhodes, while Emery Wines (*see* page 28) are produced in Embónas from locally grown grapes. White wines are made from Athiri grapes and reds from the Amorgianos varietal. **Retsina**, made from Athiri grapes, is a light, refreshingly crisp wine with only a hint of resin.

Drinks

Imported beers are expensive, while Greek lager is cheap and eminently drinkable. The most popular labels are Mythos and Hellas.

Other drinks are **ouzo**, an aniseed-based spirit that is served with iced water, which turns it milky-white. Greek **brandies** – best known among them is Metáxas – are rougher than their French counterparts, but very good when used as a base for cocktails such as Brandy Sour or Brandy Alexander.

Numerous **liqueurs** are also produced in Rhodes – some of which are very good.

Oúzeria

Oúzeria are small informal eateries whose standard fare consists of a delectable choice of *mezhédes* accompanied by *tsipouro* or *oúzo* (the two spirits are related: *tsipouro* is *oúzo's* older brother – and can be watered down if you prefer).

The routine is simple: when you have finished a round of *mezédhes*, order another if you're still hungry.

For a no-frills *oúzeri*, *see* 'Pote tin Kyriaki', page 69.

WHERE TO EAT

Where to Eat

As on the mainland, the typical Rhodian *taverna* tends to be somewhat less formal (though not necessarily cheaper) than a *estiatória* (restaurant). Touristy establishments will have menus in English and Greek. When ordering, follow the Greek custom and begin with *mezédhes* (starters). The main courses divide into meat and fish dishes. When ordering fish, bear in mind that prices are calculated by weight – half a kilo will usually be enough for two people.

A cosmopolitan range of eateries extends along the **west coast**. Around Ixiá and other coastal resorts to the west of Rhodes Town, eateries specialize in meeting the needs of the international tourist market. You'll find everything here, from pizzas and fish and chips to burgers and smorgasbord. That said, it is also possible to enjoy a traditional Greek meal, though few *tavernas* pre-date the 1960s. Many restaurants also offer live music as an accompaniment to your meal.

Tavernas, bars and fast-food outlets sit cheek by jowl on the beach roads along the **east coast**. Most offer 'international' dishes to suit their changing clientele, but there are also many good restaurants serving Greek cooking and a host of tasty traditional dishes. Check the menus and price lists carefully and, where possible, eat where the locals go to eat – that way you will be assured of the most authentic food.

In **Líndos** and the area around it, you will again notice that menus are geared to cater for an international clientele, but most restaurants do also serve authentic Greek

> **Coffee**
> Decent espresso and cappuccino can be found in Rhodes Town. Nescafé (often referred to as 'Nes') is a generic term for any kind of instant coffee in sachets, which too many hotels believe must be served with tepid water.
> Traditional Greek coffee is finely ground mocha, boiled in a small pot and served unfiltered in small cups. If you have a sweet tooth ask for *kafés glykós*, medium sweet is *métrios* and, for the hardened caffeine addict, unsweetened *skétos* or *pikrós*.
> Also very popular, and great in hot weather, is iced coffee (known as *frappé*).

Below: *A variety of restaurants can be found among the market stalls in the Old Town of Rhodes.*

Cheese

Soft *féta*, made from goats' milk and stored in brine, is the best known Greek cheese. It appears in numerous menus and has many fans in other countries. If you are buying it loose from a shop or at the market, ask to try a bit since some varieties can be very salty indeed. *Kaserí* is a hard type of cheese that is best eaten fresh, but it can also be grated – much like Parmesan.

specialities. Many of the eating establishments in the smaller towns and villages do not have a specific street address or even a published telephone number. If you wish to find an eatery or have one recommended to you – just ask the locals.

In the **interior**, there are *tavernas* in virtually every village mentioned in this book. All provide traditional Greek food, though often meat dishes only, since fish would have to be brought in from the coast. Vegetarian dishes also feature on the menus. The villages nearest Rhodes are well served with eating places: **Archipolis** has several inviting cafés and *tavernas*, while in **Embónas** most *tavernas* are geared to lunchtime coach trips.

On the **neighbouring islands**, you can often stumble upon a restaurant or *taverna* hidden in a narrow whitewashed alleyway decorated with geraniums and bougainvillea. Don't be shy, but pop in, look around and peruse the menu. The Greeks are very friendly and the proprietor will not mind.

Here, village restaurants and *tavernas* far away from the tourist track will usually be most rewarding. Also explore the islands' waterfronts. Lined with kiosks, souvláki stands, bakeries and eating places, you are sure to discover a meal to your liking here.

Below: Psistarias, *restaurants specializing in grilled meat, are sure to offer the donér kebáb, a large piece of meat cooked on a vertical spit and then carved into slices.*

Once you have found a venue that appeals, make a reservation or simply sit down and order a meal. Watch where the locals eat, as this is usually an indication that the food will be excellent, authentic Greek and reasonably priced.

Rhodes Town

Alatopipero Salt and Pepper

A bewildering array of *mezédhes* dishes and a wine list with a difference.

⊠ 76 M Petridi Street, New Town,
☎ (0241) 65-494.

Alexis Restaurant

For the best fish dishes, both traditional and unusual recipes.

⊠ 18 Odhos Sokrátous, Old Town,
☎ (0241) 29-347.

Dinoris

Good food at reasonable prices; specializes in fish dishes.

⊠ 14a Platía Moussiou, Old Town,
☎ (0241) 25-824.

Kamares

Greek and international dishes served in a traditional courtyard.

⊠ 15 Ayios Fanoúrios, Old Town,
☎ (0241) 21-337.

Les Arcs Bistro

Greek and French dishes; excellent vegetarian fare.

⊠ 16 Konstantopedos (just off Dragoumi).

Mikis Fish Grill

Famed for its fish salad.

⊠ Off Odhos Ippokratoús.

Mystagogia

Offers an enchanting initiation into mouth-watering cuisine.

⊠ Themistokleous 5,
☎ (0241) 32-981.

Myrovolos

Wonderful food, expertly prepared by an imaginative chef. Very reasonable prices.

⊠ Lahitos 13,
☎ (0241) 38-693.

Nireas

Well patronized for its excellent Greek cooking.

⊠ 22 Platía Sofokleous, Old Town,
☎ (0241) 21-703.

Palia Istoria

Imaginative Greek cooking, especially *mezédhes*. Good vegetarian selection and best quality Greek wines.

⊠ Junction of Dendrínou and Mitropóleos, New Town, ☎ (0241) 32-421.

Faliráki

Chaplin's Beach Bar

Open during the day for snacks, coffee and ice cream. At night top British DJs provide some great entertainment.

⊠ Along Faliráki's Main Beach,
☎ (0241) 85-662,
⌨ charlie@chaplins.net
⌸ www.rodos.com/chaplins

Odyssey Café-Bar

If it's a romantic evening you're after, with good music and exotic cocktails – look no further.

⊠ Faliráki Shopping Centre,
☎ (0241) 86-331.

Sting Pub

Good times and great music – this venue describes itself as 'the hottest pub in town'.

⊠ Coast Road, Faliráki,
☎ (0241) 86-891,
⌨ sting@rodos.com

Alabama Bar

Pub lunches, long drinks and a lively atmosphere, plus a large-screen TV to watch sports matches via satellite TV.
☎ (0241) 86-882.

Sarantis Restaurant

This fine establishment has been serving superb Greek and international fare, as well as some of the best Greek wines for the past 15 years.
⊠ Lindou Avenue,
☎ (0241) 85-501.

Jamaica Bar

Located in the heart of the downtown area, this bar serves English and traditional Greek breakfast, as well as a mouthwatering variety of snacks. At night the place hums with a festive crowd.
☎ (0241) 85-221.

Kings Garden Bar

Cocktail bar with British DJs, karaoke and international sports matches via satellite TV.

⊠ High Street,
☎ (0241) 85-100.

Líndos
Dionysos Taverna

Greek food on the rooftop, especially magical on moonlit nights. Reasonably priced.
⊠ In the middle of town, ☎ (0244) 31-810.

Mavrikos

Superb cooking with an interesting selection of dishes.
⊠ Main square,
☎ (0244) 31-232.

Palestra

Traditional seafood restaurant with beach views from a terrace.
⊠ Líndos Beach
☎ (0244) 31-421.

Perikles Tavernaki

Prepare pitas the traditional way.
☎ (0244) 31-767.

Gennádi
Memories

Justifiably popular – fresh fish imaginatively cooked.
⊠ Close to the beach,
☎ (0244) 43-202.

Katavía and Prasonísi

Tavernas have sprung up on the beaches: the standard fare offered is fresh fish (grilled and fried) plus grilled and spit-roast meats.

Lárdos
Maria's Restaurant

Good seafood, freshly prepared.
⊠ Village Square.

Pool House

Serves breakfast, lunch and dinner; specializes in Greek dishes.
☎ (0244) 44-322.

Roula's Taverna

Delicious Italian and Greek dishes.
⊠ Village Square.
☎ (0244) 44-300.

Péfkos
Butcher's Grill

Paradise for the carnivore – traditional village fare at reasonable prices.

Greek House

For tasty, authentic Greek cooking – both

meat and fish.

✉ *Rooftop Terrace, Main Beach Road.*

Shanghai Chinese Restaurant

Standard Chinese menu; a firm favourite with visitors who are looking for a change in diet.

To Spitaki

Traditional dishes imaginatively updated and served outside in the garden.

✉ *Main Road.*

Embónas

Two Brothers Taverna

Well worth visiting outside the busy lunch and evening periods for excellent traditional meat dishes.

☎ *(0246) 41-247.*

Chálki

Mavri Thalassa

Popular with the locals for its good fish dishes.

✉ *In the harbour,*

☎ *(0246) 45-021.*

Nissyros

Nissyros Tavern

Very popular in the

evening so be sure to arrive early.

✉ *Off Main Street,*

☎ *(0242) 31-460*

Restaurant Irini

Good traditional dishes and a small selection for vegetarians.

☎ *(0242) 31-365.*

Symi

To Hellenikon

An enormous wine cellar and superb menu have made this top restaurant justifiably famous. Pricey but well worth it.

✉ *Near Town Square,*

☎ *(0246) 72-455.*

Restaurant les Catherinettes

Very good menu – large variety of dishes.

✉ *On north side of town in the old town hall,* ☎ *(0246) 72-698.*

Tílos

To Kastro

Substantial meals very well prepared. Some spontaneous entertainment at night.

✉ *On the southern side of the village,*

☎ *(0246) 44-232.*

Kárpathos

Mike's

Tasty Greek fare.

✉ *Apodimon Kárpathou, Pigádia,*

☎ *(0245) 22-727.*

Café Kárpathos

For those in need of good coffee and tasty sandwiches.

✉ *Apodimon Kárpathou, Pigádia.*

To Helleniko

In- and outdoor dining. Serves Kárpathian specialities such as *stifado* (meat stew with tomato and onion sauce).

✉ *Apodimon Kárpathou, Pigádia.*

Kos

Petrino Restaurant

In- and outdoor dining; has an excellent menu.

✉ *Plateia Ioannou Theologou,*

☎ *(0242) 27-251.*

Pote tin Kyriaki

Experience a typical *oúzeri* (see page 64).

✉ *Pisandrou 9,*

☎ *(0242) 27-872,*

🕒 *Mon–Sat.*

Above: *Neoclassical houses cling to the hillside above Yiálos harbour on Sými.*

Detour to Turkey
There are very good inter-island connections in the main season. Proximity to the coast of Turkey makes a day trip there convenient (albeit expensive). (*See page 83.*)
Please note: visitors with charter flight tickets cannot stay in Turkey overnight under any circumstances. If they do, their return ticket becomes invalid.

EXCURSIONS

The neighbouring islands can be visited either en route to Rhodes by ferry from Athens (Piraeus), or on a day trip as part of an island-hopping itinerary that begins on Rhodes.

The influence of successive rulers, from Venetian to Ottoman and Italian, has given the islands a distinctive character and architecture. Incidentally, the name **Dodecanese** (12 islands) is a misnomer – it is the number of islands mentioned in Byzantine times, and the name stuck but there are about 16 inhabited islands and several bare rocks.

Rhodes is both the administrative and economic centre of the Prefecture but the islands are often considered as two groups: northern and southern Dodecanese centred on Kos and Rhodes respectively. **Kos** is second only to Rhodes as a tourist magnet. **Chálki** and **Níssyros**, untouched by mass tourism, offer a complete contrast to Kos yet could not be more different: Chálki is an arid limestone outcrop devoid of any natural water supply, while Níssyros – one of the few volcanic islands – is fertile with dark sands and hot springs.

Wild, unspoiled **Kárpathos**, the second largest of the group, has a superb coastline and is a mass of wildflowers in spring; **Sými**, having little water, must restrict visitors and, like **Tílos**, has an air of exclusivity.

CHÁLKI

Chálki

An intriguing, unspoiled island, Chálki is friendly and uncompromisingly Greek. The largest of the islands off the west coast of Rhodes, it is a barren rock and its (distinctly 'brackish') water supply comes in tankers from Rhodes. This means that tourist numbers cannot grow too large and the island is perfect for escape and relaxation.

In the olden days copper ore was mined on the island (*chálkis* means copper) and at the beginning of the 20th century sponge fishing created the island's wealth. The supply of **sea sponges** died out and there was mass emigration to Florida. Funds from émigres built the main road out of the harbour – Boulevard Tarpon Springs (from the name in Florida).

Embório, the main settlement on Chálki, is the prime focus for daytrippers: **Ayios Nikólaos church** boasts a tall campanile, while a row of ruined **windmills** guards the harbour.

Italianate houses that were built by wealthy fishermen cling to the hillside. Restored and painted in soft pastel colours – reminder of a failed venture to make the island an international youth centre – many are now available for rent by tourists. The village has four *tavernas*, as many bars and a genuine *oúzerie*.

Chálki
Location: Map E–B1
Distance from Rhodes: 20km (12 miles)

Travelling by Ferry
A **daily ferry** linking Rhodes with Chálki leaves from Kámiros Skála, every day around 12:30, returning the following morning. On Sundays there's a **round trip** leaving around 09:00, otherwise using the ferry means staying on Chálki. In summer **day trips** to Chálki leave from Kámiros Skála: Lack of available rooms can create problems in high season.

Below: *Today, most sponge is imported at high cost.*

71

Póndamos, reached along the Boulevard Tarpon Springs, has the island's only sandy **beach**. Nevertheless, crystal clear waters around the island make this a paradise for **snorkelling**. Yiali, Arous and Kania can easily be reached on foot via rough paths – an excursion boat from Emborío takes you further afield to Areta or Trachia.

Chálki is almost traffic-free and ideal for visitors who have come in search of solitude. There are good walking opportunities – one crosses the stark landscape en route to the monastery of **Ayios Ioánnis Pródhromos** where you can stay overnight.

Chorió, the island's deserted settlement and old town, is closer and now just 5km (3 miles) away via a new road. It comes to life for the festival of the Assumption of the Blessed Virgin Mary held on 15 August each year at the frescoed church of the Panayía. High above Chorió there are remains of a fortress built on an ancient acropolis: on a clear day both Kárpathos and Crete are visible on the horizon.

Below: *Chálki offers a haven for visitors who want to get away from it all.*

If you are planning to stay on Chálki for a while, it is worth taking an excursion by boat to **Alimnía**. This abandoned islet is very much greener than Chálki and has some superb beaches. The ruined fortress on Alimnía is reminiscent of past occupation and is fun to explore.

Níssyros

The landscape of the only volcanic island in the Dodecanese contrasts with the bare limestone of the other islands in the group. Volcanic soils are rich in minerals and retain water even in a dry climate, so Níssyros is green and lush.

Most visitors come here on a day trip to see the volcanic wastelands in the island's centre. If you're planning on staying a few days, the local morning bus to Nikiá allows more time to explore. From the village, the walk into the **caldera** takes about half an hour. The biggest of the five **craters** in the caldera is some 350m (1148ft) wide and 25m (82ft) deep. Some houses in **Embório**, the other village on the caldera rim, were damaged during the last eruption, but are now being restored.

Island life centres on Mandráki, which serves as both port and capital – a short walk from the harbour takes you to the Langadáki district where there is a maze of lanes, many paved with traditional pebble mosaics. Many of the brightly painted houses follow a distinctive design, tall and rather narrow, with balconies.

A fortress (Kástro) stands above Mandráki harbour. It was built by the Knights of St John in 1315. Within the walls is the island's **Historical and Popular Museum** and a cave with the 15th-century monastery church of **Panayía Spilianí**. On the hills above the Kástro lie remains of huge 'Cyclopean' walls of the Paliokástro, cut from the volcanic rock and part of the Dorian acropolis.

Above: *The lunar landscape of a volcanic crater on the island of Níssyros.*

Níssyros
Location: Map H–C2
Distance from Rhodes: 80km (50 miles)

Visitor information:
🖳 www.nisyros.com
Níssyrian Travel,
☎ (0242) 31-204.

Transport
Ferry services:
G&A Ferries,
☎ (0246) 71-230;
DANE Sea Lines,
☎ (0246) 71-307;
Hydrofoil services:
to Rhodes on Sat & Sun
(around 2 hours).
Catamaran services:
Sea Star connects
Níssyros, Tílos and
Rhodes daily.
Bus services: At least
two tours to the volcanoes every day. Tickets
at Mandráki harbour.
Taxi service: Babis,
☎ (0242) 31-460.

Above: *Sými's lovely location makes it a popular destination.*

Sými

The trip from Rhodes to Sými is worth it just for the view of Yiálos port when the ferry nears the island. In the day, large numbers of daytrippers invade the lower part of the town. If you wish to escape the crush, walk up to the castle via **Kalí Strata** (357 steps), or visit the beach. A degree of normality returns when the trip boats depart, leaving yachtsmen of every nationality to enjoy the harbour.

The climb up Kalí Strata to **Chorió**, a delightful village with narrow streets and whitewashed cuboid houses, is to take a step back in time. There is a 19th-century pharmacy here, and the churches of **Ayios Panteleímon** and **Ayios Giórgios**, as well as a **museum** with a collection of local finds. Higher up sits the **Kástro**, where Byzantine walls, built from the earlier classical settlement, were later fortified by the Knights and given the coat of arms of Grand Master d'Aubusson (*see page 19*) The acropolis was once the site of a temple dedicated to Aphrodite.

In spring and again in September and October the island is truly idyllic, but July and August bring the crowds, and the enclosed nature of the harbour can make it unbearably hot and humid.

Sými

In ancient times Sými was famed for the quality of its boat building – its shipwrights built the *Argo* for **Jason and the Argonauts** and this skill was revived under the rule of the Knights; the Turks also used the speedy *skafés* (skiffs) in raids.

Locals grew rich on the profits of a thriving sponge fishing industry and built their mansions in tiers above the harbour. Süleyman saw an advantage in allowing the islanders a measure of independence (and permission to dive in Turkish waters) in return for an annual tribute of the best sponges. The economy floundered, however, with the coming of the steam ship and as a result of the 'sponge blight' of the early 20th century (*see page 72*). Today the population is but a tenth of what it once was. Imported sponges are still on sale down near the harbour, along with local herbs and knicknacks at a plethora of stalls geared to attract daytrippers.

Walkers will come across numerous tiny churches on Sými (77 in total), many of them near delightful secluded coves and most of them dedicated to the Archangel Michael. The large and wealthy **Monastery of Taxiárchis Michael Panormítis** (patron saint of sailors), in the south of the island, is popular with daytrippers (boat trips from Rhodes include it with Yiálos) and with Greek pilgrims worldwide, especially the sailors who invoke the saint's protection with votive offerings of precious metals. Visitors can rent a cell and stay at the monastery if they wish. From the monastery a trail leads through the woods to **Marathoúnda Bay** – attractive, but not as picturesque as **Nánou Bay** to the north across the headland.

Sými
Location: Map H–E2
Distance from Rhodes:
35km (22 miles)
🖳 www.symi-island.gr

Visitor information:
ANES ticket office,
✉ Northern side of harbour.

Local Museum:
🕐 Tue–Sun
10:00–14:00.

Police:
☎ (0246) 71-111.

Port police:
☎ (0246) 71-205.

Ferry services:
Not as well served as other islands.
G&A Ferries,
☎ (0246) 71-230;
DANE Sea Lines,
☎ (0246) 71-307, have two ferries each week, heading north.

Hydrofoil services:
Aigli leaves Sými for Rhodes early in the morning and returns in the evening (check daily schedule).

Catamaran services:
Dodekanisos Express (based in Rhodes) docks at Sými on weekends in summer.

Bus services:
Minibus service from Gialos to Pedi.

Taxi services:
The island has four taxis – check with the Visitor Information office.

Tílos

Tílos
Location: Map H–C3
Distance from Rhodes:
65km (40 miles)

Visitor information:
Tílos Travel Agency:
✉ On the waterfront,
☎ (0246) 44-259.
Ferry: G&A Ferries,
☎ (0246) 71-230;
DANE Sea Lines,
☎ (0246) 71-307.
Hydrofoil: to Rhodes
Wed and Sun afternoon.
Catamaran: *Sea Star*
daily en route to
Nissyros and Rhodes.
Bus: one minibus and
bus on daily schedules.
Taxi: two taxis – check
with the Visitor
Information office.

According to Greek mythology, Tílos was named after the youngest son of the sun god Helios and his wife, Alia. The boy came to the island in search of medicinal plants to cure his ailing mother. Tílos' fame in antiquity came from perfume produced here, and also as the birthplace of the poetess Erinna (4th century BC). Under Roman rule the island was largely forgotten but the Knights of St John took over its administration in 1309 and began building a series of seven fortresses.

Somehow, Tílos has escaped the ravages of tourism. Enthusiastic walkers and bird-watchers have certainly discovered it but kept the secret.

The capital, **Megálo Chorió**, is known to have been inhabited by Minoans and then Mycenaeans. In the 3rd century BC it allied with Rhodes, but in 225BC an earthquake destroyed its walls and temples. Today, it is a delightful village – so typical of the Mediterranean – full of colourful flowers in summer. There is a Venetian Kástro artfully constructed out of stones from ancient Tílos, incorporating a gateway that once stood on the site. The church, dedicated to the Archangel Michael, has icons from an earlier church built inside the Kástro. **Livádia**, the port, is the only other inhabited village (there were once nine). It is

Below: *Dovecotes are an appealing feature on the Dodecanese islands.*

very popular with Greek families and its *tavernas* produce good local dishes. Livádia has a long shingle beach with a crystal clear sea. There are several pretty churches near the waterfront – **Ayios Nikólaos**, and further along the road towards the

Above: *Red pantiled roofs can be seen on churches in Tílos.*

beach, an early Christian basilica, **Ayios Panteleímon**. Around the coast from the port are two more good **pebble beaches** at Lethrá and at Armókosti.

Mikró Chorió, now uninhabited, is worth walking to, both for incredible views en route and for its old churches – **Ayios Elesas** and **Ayios Sotiras** have 15th-century frescoes, while the old church of **Timia Zóni** has frescoes dating from the 18th century. Below the town there is a long sandy beach at Eristos.

In 1971 a ravine near **Mikró Chorió** (the grotto of Hercadio) yielded a wealth of animal bones along with Stone-Age pottery fragments. The bones were identified as those of deer, tortoise and mastodon from the Pleistocene era 10,000 ago, when the island became detached from the mainland.

The best **walk** on Tílos is the 8km (5 mile) route from Megálo Chorió to the fortified Byzantine Monastery of Ayios Panteleímon (15th century) built high above the coast. The frescoes are in poor condition but the view makes the climb worthwhile. From 25–26 July each year the island's biggest festival, Feast of Agios Pandeleimonas, is held here.

> **Proud Traditions**
>
> Older women of Tílos often wear elaborate traditional costumes. The island's dances are unique and there is a repertoire of ancient songs linked to the many festivals celebrated here. During a festival from 25–26 July and again on 8 November, women perform the **Dance of the Cup** in the courtyard of the Church of Archangel Michael in Megálo Chorió. Mikró Chorió bursts into life for the *panayíri* celebrating the Assumption of Virgin Mary on 15 August.

EXCURSIONS

Kárpathos

Kárpathos, with its wild land-scape, is still quiet and unspoiled, even though it boasts a new international airport. With two **mountains** over 1000m (3281ft) high and superb wild flowers, it is a paradise for walkers and naturalists, and the extensive **beaches** with white sands are often empty.

A lot of people come to Kárpathos on a day trip to visit the village of **Olympos** high in the mountains.

Above: *Traditional costumes are worn at festival times.*

In spite of being a popular attraction, Diafáni is still a treasure house of graceful old buildings and aging windmills. From **Diafáni** you can also take a Sunday boat trip to the islet of **Sariá**, which forms the northern tip of Kárpathos.

Northern Kárpathos is separated from the south by mountainous terrain. A 12km (7½ mile) track, which can be traversed by four-wheel-drive vehicle or on foot, leads southward from Olympos to Spoa through dramatic scenery. However, visitors bound for **Pigádia** travel by caïque from Diafáni, or visit direct on boats from Rhodes.

Pigádia, the capital of Kárpathos island, is an uncompromisingly Greek town situated in **Vróntis Bay** – a one-time pirate cove. This was the site of ancient Kárpathos, a city dedicated to Poseidon, god of the sea. Vróntis Bay has a fine stretch of sand to the north of Pigádia town and there are several good hotels, a few tavernas and some interesting churches, including the remains of columns denoting the site of an early Christian basilica named **Ayia Fotiní**.

Kárpathos
Location: Map H–C5
Distance from Rhodes:
75km (47 miles)

Tourist Information office, Pigadia:
✉ Harbourfront
☎ (0245) 23-835
📠 (0245) 23-836
🖥 www.karpathos.com
🍴 Good restaurants at Pigadia harbourfront.
Air travel: flights daily from Athens & Rhodes.
Ferry: F/B Vitsentzos-Kornaros and F/B Lerapetra call at Kárpathos three times a week from Rhodes.
Bus: bus schedule at the airport.
Taxi rank: ☎ (0245) 22-705, on Dimokratias, in Pigadia.

78

The main tourist resort is at **Ammopí** south of Vróntis beach. To the north, regular caïques leave Pigádia for the superb beaches of **Kyrá Panayía** and **Apélla**, set at the foot of dramatic **Mt Kalilimni** (1188m; 3898ft), the highest in the Dodecanese.

Arkássa on the west coast is surrounded by fruit groves. A track to the southwest leads to the site of ancient Arkássa. For the explorer there are caves along the coast and remains of early Christian churches with mosaic flooring, such as **Ayia Sofia** and **Ayia Anastásia**. The coast north of Arkássa is rocky and the sea can be rough but there are attractive coves along the coast. One of them, **Finíki**, is a pretty fishing village. From here caïques travel to Kássos – southernmost of the Dodecanese islands.

A narrow road encircles Mt Profítis Ilías, passing through villages perched high on hillsides. The route takes in Menetés, Pilés, Othos, at 450m (1477ft) the highest on Kárpathos, and Volada. Both **Menetés** and **Othos** have a craft museum. **Apéri**, the last village before the road returns to Pigádia, was once capital and is regarded as one of Greece's richest villages, since many expatriates have built houses there.

Olympos
Isolation has enabled the village of Olympos to remain a repository of ancient traditions and crafts. Bread and delicious vegetable pies are baked in outdoor ovens while two mills in the wonderfully photogenic line of windmills above the village still grind corn for flour. Isolation for centuries has also preserved a unique local dialect with traces of Dorian and Phrygian languages, laws governing female inheritance and traditional melodies played on lyre and *tsamboúna*.

Below: *Some of the most rugged and dramatic terrain in the Dodecanese is found on Kárpathos.*

EXCURSIONS

Kos

Its central location on ferry routes makes Kos an excellent starting point for island hopping.

The ancients liked its position too, and Kos was continuously occupied by successive civilizations from 3500BC. In classical times Kos had close links with Halicarnassus (Bodrum in Turkey) and was a member of the Dorian Hexapolis (*see page 83*).

Kardaména, the most popular resort after Kos town, has developed beyond recognition. There's a Club Med site between **Kamári** and the far southwest where beaches are excellent. At **Ayios Stéfanos** there is a superb early Christian basilica looking out to the islet of Kastri. Inland, **Ayios Pávlos** and Ayios Ioánnis are two Byzantine basilicas near Zipári on the road to Asfendíou. **Ziá**, a popular tourist village, makes a good base for ascents of **Mt Orómedon**, whose peak Díkaios Christos (685m; 2248ft) is the highest on Kos.

Kos Town

In spite of mass tourism, Kos town has retained its charm. The town square, Platía Eleftherías, is dominated by the **Defterdar Mosque**, still in use today. Here you can also find the museum, the municipal fruit market

Kos
Location: Map H–C1
Distance from Rhodes: 100km (62 miles)

Visitor information:
✉ Vasileos Georgiou 1, Kos Town, ☎ (0242) 24-460; 🖶 (0242) 21-111, 🖰 dotkos@hol.gr 🖥 www.hippocrates.gr 🕐 08:00–20:00 Mon–Fri and 08:00–15:00 weekends (May–Oct).
Air travel: three flights daily to Athens.
Ferry: G&A Ferries, ☎ (0242) 28-545; DANE Sea Lines, ☎ (0242) 27-311, and F/B Nisos-Kalymnos, ☎ (0242) 28-545.
Hydrofoil: Kyriacoulis ☎ (0242) 25-920.
Catamaran: Dodekanisos Express daily from Rhodes in high season.
Bus station: ✉ Kleopatras 7, Kos Town, ☎ (0242) 22-292.
Taxi rank: ✉ Akti Koundourioti, Kos Town.

Below: *Dramatic sunset over Kardaména village on Kos.*

(**Agorá**) and **Porta tou Forou** (the gate to the ancient Agorá). **Gazi Hassan Pasha Mosque** was built by the Turks in 1786 to overlook the supposedly ancient plane tree under which Hippocrates is said to have taught. The Turks also installed a fountain under it with an ancient sarcophagus as a basin. The Castle of the Knights was built from stones of the Agorá. Grand Master d'Aubusson rebuilt the walls and added extra buildings after an earthquake in 1495.

Above: *Tall columns mark the boundary of the Roman Odeion on Kos.*

Roman Ruins

Most of the Roman remains lie on either side of **Grigoríou Street**. Down Tsaldári Street is the **stadium**. Close to the Olympic Airways office is the **Altar of Dionysos**, and nearby, hidden in a concrete building, **Casa Romana** – a house with mosaics and baths that was destroyed in an earthquake in AD554. Italian archaeologists did much work in the **acropolis** and **forum** just behind the bus station. They also uncovered the main **Roman highway**.

The Asklepeíon

The Asklepeíon in the hills southwest of Kos town was perhaps the most famous centre of healing in the ancient world, built some time after Hippocrates' death (c. 377BC). It is set on four terraces. At the lowest are the Roman Baths (3rd century AD). On the second level lies the entrance, a spring and a small temple. Temples to Apollo and Asklepiós stood on the third level, and on the fourth a Doric Temple to Asklepiós constructed in the 2nd century BC.

> **Brief history of Kos**
> Hippocrates, the father of medicine, was born on Kos; the Ptolemies of Egypt sent their sons to be educated there and the Romans valued the island for its production of silk. Persian and Saracen pirates made frequent raids until the Knights of St John took over in 1315. After the fall of Rhodes to Süleyman in AD1522, the Turks took over Kos, but by treaty rather than force. Severe earthquakes have bedevilled successive civilizations on Kos, the latest in 1933.

Above: *For a real slice of Turkish life visit Marmaris on market days.*

The Turkish Coast

The legendary enmity between Greek and Turk is certainly not apparent when you visit Marmaris – nothing gets in the way of good business. If you have flown to Rhodes by charter flight remember this: stay overnight in Turkey and your ticket is no longer valid. This is to prevent Turkish tourism getting a boost from cheap flights to Greece. No restriction applies to scheduled flights.

Ferry trips to Marmaris are expensive. Greek tax is included in the ticket price – Turkish tax is paid on arrival. Passports must be handed in to the ferry company the day before departure. Most tourist agencies on Rhodes can organize the trip.

Marmaris

Marmaris was reconstructed after an earthquake in 1957 and is now a popular resort. Its marina has approximately 800 berths and the setting is superb – the town is located in a long bay fringed by pine trees and oleander bushes that burst into pink bloom in summer.

The old quarter is built on a rocky peninsula that surrounds a 16th-century Ottoman citadel. The main **shopping area** of Marmaris lies in side streets running off Republic Square (Cumhuriyet Meydani) and Atatürk Square. Salesmen are very persistent but friendly – some carpet sellers could probably sell sand to Arabs after pioneering ice-cream sales to the Inuit. **Bazaar 54** near the marina is a reliable company, and **Silk Road** another which can handle exports with ease. For a meal look no further than the restaurants around the harbour.

If you have a scheduled flight and decide to spend a day or more in Turkey, there are taxi boats from Marmaris around the coast to the town of **Datça** which is located on a long narrow peninsula. Some boats continue to **Knidos**, the ancient city at the end of the peninsula – once part of the Dorian Hexapolis (*see* page 80) and famed for its wine. For those interested in visiting all these sites, local boats ply between Rhodes– Marmaris–Datça–Bodrum–Kos and back to Rhodes, but the trip is pricey.

Bodrum

Visitors to Rhodes who also intend to include a few days in Kos on their trip can arrange to go to Bodrum in Turkey – the site of ancient Halicarnassus where King Mausolus built his tomb, one of the wonders of the ancient world, and thereby giving us the word 'mausoleum'. The remains lie near the imposing Medieval **Castle of St Peter**. This castle, built by the Knights of St John, again made unsentimental use of stonework from the ancient city.

Today, the castle is the home of Bodrum's famous museum which displays not only some of the very oldest shipwrecks in the world, but also interesting exhibits of their cargoes, such as glass vessels, earthenware jars and more.

Turkish Travel Tips
A day trip to Turkey is relatively easy to accomplish. Ferry connections, especially in season, are abundant. Do bear in mind, however, that this is an expensive exercise – you'll have to pay for the fare as well as Turkish port taxes. Also remember that bookings need to be made in advance, so that your passport details can be checked. A single day trip does not require a visa, but you'll require one if you wish to extend your stay. Be aware that leather items, carpets and other good-value buys may attract the attention of Greek customs officials, who may decide to levy import tax.

Below: *Beautiful Turkish rugs and kelims for sale.*

Above: *Ayios Nikólaos fort and the Platóni are landmarks at the entrance to Mandráki harbour.*

Best Times to Visit

In the summer months (June–September), the Old Town of **Rhodes** can be crowded and very hot during the day although evenings are pleasant. The light is much softer during February–April and in October, bringing the best out in the architecture. Sunny winter days and good facilities make a winter holiday memorable. The **western resorts**, although crowded in summer, are very well-equipped and the *meltémi* makes the heat more tolerable. The larger hotels cater for a year-round trade. From February to April the flowers are at their best and in October the sea is still pleasantly warm. From June–September **east coast resorts** are full of pleasure-seeking visitors: safe swimming makes resorts ideal for families. In spring and autumn the dramatic coast from **Tsambíka** to **Líndos** is great for walking, and flowers offer a spring bonus. **Líndos** is extremely popular from June–September with package holiday-makers and day visitors; it is also very hot. Outside the tourist season Líndos offers a charming escape – the hills around are filled with flowers in spring, and the Easter celebrations are famous worldwide. Walkers can enjoy the **mountains** in the interior all year – but it can get surprisingly cold in the winter months (November–March). In summer the higher ground offers a welcome escape from coastal crowds and high temperatures. Flowers are best from March to late May. Unfortunately, the smaller islands – **Chálki, Níssyros, Tílos** and **Sými** – almost close for business in winter. Ferries become irregular, but persistent visitors will usually be able to get by. **Kos**, like Rhodes, is a year-round resort.

Tourist Information

The **National Tourist Organization of Greece** (EOT or NTOG) produces a range of free brochures and accommodation directories dealing with the major islands (Crete, Rhodes, Corfu) and island groups. **London**, ✉ 195 Regent Street, W1, ☎ (020) 7734-5997, 📠 (020) 7287-1369. **New York**, ✉ Olympic Tower, 645 Fifth Avenue, fifth floor, NY 10022, ☎ (212) 421 5777, 📠 (212) 826-6940. **Chicago**, ✉ 168 N. Michigan Ave, Illinois. 60601, ☎ (312) 782 1084, 📠 (312) 782 1091. **California**, ✉ 611 West 6th St, Suite 2198, LA, CA 90017, ☎ (213) 626 6696, 📠 (213) 489 9744. **Athens**, ✉ 2 Amerikís St, Athens 10564, ☎ (01) 322-3111, 📠 (01) 322-2841. **Rhodes Town**, ✉ cnr Alexandrou Papágou & Makaríou streets, ☎ (0241) 23-255, 📠 (0241) 26-955. **City of Rhodes Tourist Information Centre**, Son et Lumière Square, ☎ (0241) 35-945. **Líndos**, ☎ (0244)

31-428. *Rodos News* is a free, local paper with information on bus and ferry timetables, as well as restaurant listings and happenings.

Entry Requirements

From 1995 EU citizens can stay on Rhodes indefinitely; most other visitors (including those from Australia, Canada, New Zealand and USA) are allowed up to three months (South Africans: two months), no visas are required. Children must either hold their own passports or be entered in parental passports. **Visa extensions** or **work permits** can be obtained from the **Aliens Bureau**, ✉ Leforos Alexandras 173, 11522 Athens, Greece, ☎ (01) 770-5711. **Temporary jobs**, including work in bars and restaurants, are not difficult to find on Rhodes. Graduates who are hoping to find jobs teaching English will need a **TEFL qualification**.

Customs

Visitors arriving from **EU countries** can import duty-free no more than 400g of tobacco (300 cigarettes or 75 cigars), 5 litres of wine or 1.5 litres of spirits, 75 grams of perfume or other articles of value up to a total of 160 Euro. If you are arriving from non–EU countries these allowances are reduced to 250 grams of tobacco (200 cigarettes), 2 litres of wine or 1 litre of alcoholic beverage, 50 grams of perfumes and gifts to a value of 20 Euro.

Health Requirements

No certificates of vaccination are required for visitors.

Getting There

By Air: Direct scheduled flights operate daily to Athens from London and New York (less frequently from Montreal and Toronto) and, in season, to Rhodes and the larger islands which have international airports (Crete, Corfu, Kos, Lésbos, Mýkonos, Skiáthos, Zákinthos). Operators to Athens include TWA, Olympic, BA and Virgin Atlantic.

In summer there are numerous charter flights direct to Rhodes from UK, German and Scandinavian airports. Athens has two airports, 10 minutes' drive apart, one of which is served only by flights of **Olympic Airways** (four a day to Rhodes). **Aegean Air** and **Cronus Airlines** use the other one. All flights arrive at and depart from Rhodes' **Ellinikon Airport's** west terminal. East terminal serves all other international and charter fights. Rhodes airport is situated at Paradíssi 16km (10 miles) southwest of Rhodes Town. **Charter flights** are met by coaches working for the tour operators. The choice for independent travellers is: public bus service, taxi or Olympic

Airways bus (tickets from Olympic desk inside airport) from Olympic Airways office at 9 Odhos Lerou Lochou, Rhodes Town. Departures from this stop around 90 minutes before flight time. **Restrictions on charter flights** mean validity for a minimum of three days and maximum of six weeks – you must have an accommodation voucher stating the name and address of destination, even if mythical. Charter passengers can only visit a neighbouring country (**Turkey**) for a day and not overnight, otherwise the ticket is invalidated: Turkish officials will stamp a piece of paper to avoid putting a Turkish stamp in your passport. This applies to current visits only: there is no problem with previous trips to Turkey.

By Road: Routes by car all centre on Athens. From Athens there are regular car ferries to

Rhodes. Buses from many European countries travel to Athens. Passengers transfer to ferries or charter flights to reach Rhodes. Due to strife in former Yugoslavia, **buses** from London to Athens go via Italy and the ferry to Greece, taking three days. Contact **Olympic Bus Ltd**, ⊠ 70 Brunswick Centre, London WC1 1AE, ☎ (020) 7837-9141. **By Rail:** Direct trains from London to Athens are no longer available, but it is possible to make a rail journey through Italy, via Paris and Bologna to Brindisi and take the ferry from there to Patras. **British Rail International**, ☎ (0845) 748-4950. **By Boat:** There are daily ferries between Rhodes and Piraeus (or Rafína), tickets available from the ferry company offices. If you intend to interrupt your journey, you must purchase a ticket for each section of the trip separately. Rhodes lies on a number of ferry routes, permitting easy links with Astipálaia, Chálki, Crete, Folégandros, Kálimnos, Kárpathos, Kássos, Kastellórhizo, Kos, Léros, Lipsí, Mílos, Níssyros, Páros, Pátmos, Sífnos, Sými, Syros, Thíra and Tílos. Connections from Kos allow ferry and hydrofoil links with other island groups as well as Chíos, Lésbos and Sámos and northern mainland ports Kavála and Alexandroúpolis. **International ferries** connect with Cyprus (Limassol) and Italy (Venice), thus sparing visitors who choose to bring their own cars from Europe the journey down to Athens. In general, **hydrofoils** begin to operate in May and are twice as fast as conventional ferries, but double the price. **Ferry timetables** change annually. The best source of information is the ***Athens Gazette*** (on sale in all bookshops and kiosks in Athens).

What to Pack

In summer, cotton T-shirts and shorts suffice most of the time. Out of season, however, the evenings can be cool and a pullover (even waterproofs) make good sense. In the more up-market resorts you might want slightly more elegant clothes for the evening, but leave the tuxedo at home. Hats, sunglasses and UV protection suncream are advisable during the day.

Money Matters

Currency: With effect from January 2002, the Euro replaces the drachma, with notes in denominations of 5, 10, 20, 50, 100, 200 and 500 Euros. Coins come in 1, 2, 5, 10, 20 and 50 Euro cents and 1 and 2 Euros.

Currency exchange: Other than on the remotest islands there is always some means of changing money in a bank (*trápeza*), post office or even the shipping agent. Post offices

<u>Out of season</u>
Henry Miller, Lawrence Durrell and many other writers have travelled to the islands to complete a 'great work'. Larger islands such as Rhodes and Crete can cater for tourists all year round but small islands literally close shop during the winter months and are difficult to reach. If you do decide to make it to Rhodes out of season, however, attempt a few words of Greek: you will be welcomed as a traveller rather than a tourist – Greeks are marvellous at spotting the difference.

TRAVEL TIPS

Risky Business
Cautionary tales abound of people who were seduced by a holiday into trying to run a business in Greece. If you feel like attempting the same, remember that rules, regulations and laws are a minefield made for Greeks by Greeks. It can work if you have a Greek partner, preferably linked by marriage!

Below: *During the Easter procession, an icon is carried from the monastery at Moní Skiádi through villages to the coast and on to Chálki.*

change cash, traveller's cheques and Euro-cheques, and also charge less commission than the banks do. In the bigger resorts, the numbers of ACTs (automatic cash tellers) grow yearly.

Traveller's cheques: Thomas Cook and American Express are accepted in all banks and post offices (you need your passport as ID). Cash transfers are best handled by major banks in Athens, or in Rhodes Town.

Credit Cards: allow withdrawals at banks and ACTs. **Visa** is handled by the Commercial bank of Greece; and **Access/Mastercard** by the National Bank.

Tipping: Although a 10–15% service charge is added to restaurant bills, Greeks generally leave change as a tip. Taxi drivers, porters and cleaners welcome a tip; the amount depends on the service.

VAT: 6%, 13% or 18%, depending on service or product provided.

Transport

Boat: Inter-island services are operated by ferry and hydrofoil (rough seas can play havoc with hydrofoil schedules). To smaller islands there are **caïque services** and **taxi boats** operating between ports, resorts and other beaches. Always check the ferry times with the local port authority and book from the boat's central agency where possible.

Road: Bus services on Rhodes are better than on most Greek islands. Most villages and all resorts are accessible from Rhodes Town. Bus services operate roughly half-hourly from the Néa Agorá area. For east coast resorts – Platía Rimini. For west coast resorts – Averof Street. An hourly service goes to inland villages and several times a day to the far south. Throughout summer there is an express service to Líndos.

TRAVEL TIPS

Taxis: are a widely used form of transport on all the islands – be sure to agree on a price before the journey, or make sure the meter is running. Sharing is common practice – each person pays full rate for the part of the journey they undertake.
For 24-hour **radiocabs**, ☎ (0241) 64-712, 64-757, or 64-734.

Cars: Charges and fuel costs are very high in Greece: the best deals come as part of a 'fly-drive'. For exploring, a car is a useful option, but check for any damage on your vehicle (especially brakes and a spare wheel) before you set out. Check what the insurance covers (usually tyres and underbody damage are excluded). Non–EU citizens need an **International Driving Licence**.
Always pay the supplement for the collision-damage waiver to avoid potential problems. Assistance can be sought from the

Automobile and Touring Club of Greece (ELPA) in Rhodes Town, 104. If you do have the misfortune to be involved in an accident, contact the **Tourist Police**, ☎ (0241) 27-423 Rhodes, ☎ 92-219 Triánda, ☎ 51-222 Afándou.

Car hire outlets for Budget, Europe Car, Eurodollar, Avis and Hertz operate at airports and in Rhodes Town. If you take your car to Greece, one year's free use is permitted by customs (with a four-month extension on request) – North American and Australian citizens are allowed two years.

Motorcycles, Bicycles and Scooters: are a cheap and cheerful way of travelling. Check the machine carefully first (particularly brakes), wear protective clothing and bring a helmet.

Business Hours

The opening hours vary according to the nature of the business and are often quite confusing, even for Greeks. For essential goods try between 08:30 and 13:30 – if a shop opens for the afternoon it will usually be for the hours 16:30–20:00. In popular tourist resorts shops tend to stay open continuously until 22:00.

Banking hours: Banks are open 08:00–14:00 Monday–Friday.

Sites: Most museums and archaeological sites are closed on Mondays, but otherwise open daily from 09:00–15:00. At Kámiros and Líndos, sites close at 17:00 (19:00 in summer).

Time Difference

Greece is two hours ahead of Greenwich Mean Time, one hour ahead of Central European Time and seven hours ahead of US Standard Winter Time. Clocks go forward one hour in the last March weekend, and back on the last Sunday in September.

Communications

Post: There are post offices (*tachidromío*) and money changing facilities in all large and small towns and at all ports. They all provide normal postal services (also including poste restante). English is often spoken. Post can be slow (up to three weeks for a card). Express mail, though more expensive, is also much faster. Stamps (*grammatósima*) are sold at kiosks and at tourist shops; post boxes are bright yellow.

Telephones: If you need to make an international call, you can do so from your hotel, or more cheaply from any of the OTE offices (*Organismós Telefikoinonía Elládos*) – there's at least one on every island allowing you to dial direct or make collect calls. For the UK dial 0044, then the area code (omitting the zero at the beginning); for the US dial 001. **Cardphones** have now replaced payphones everywhere – **phonecards** are sold at *periptera*. You have a much better chance of getting through from Rhodes to Athens in the evenings – wait for a series of six clicks that are audible after the area code to reduce the chances of having to redial endlessly.

Electricity

The mains voltage is 220AC supplied at 50Hz. Plugs are continental 2-pin – universal adaptors fit them. All US appliances need converters.

Weights and Measures

The metric system is generally used throughout Rhodes.

Health Precautions

Visitors to the islands should make sure that their **tetanus** protection is up to date. Don't underestimate the strength of the **sun** – even short exposures to sensitive skins can leave a child or adult in agony for days afterward. Use wide-rimmed sun hats, dark sunglasses, a high-protection factor sun screen and do practise sensible sunbathing, avoiding overexposure.

Excessive olive oil can cause **stomach upsets** – retsina, Coca-Cola and fresh parsley (*mitanós*) can help. Carry your own toilet paper. **Tap water** is safe to drink – bottled water is widely available on Rhodes.

Health services

There is a reciprocal agreement giving free medical treatment to **EU residents** (UK visitors should take form E111 from the DHSS). Make sure your travel insurance offers medical cover plus the provision of an 'air taxi' in emergencies. Many doctors speak English but equipment in some Greek hospitals is often behind what is commonplace at home.

TRAVEL TIPS

Personal Safety

Theft is still not very commonplace on the island of Rhodes, but has increased in recent years. Generally, any harassment of lone females is low-key outside tourist resorts and many women do explore the island alone – a sharp *fíyete* (go away) or *afístime* (leave me alone) usually suffices to discourage unwanted attention. (Greek friends may equip you with some more forceful phrases.) Much has been made in the western press about incidents of rape – they horrify Greeks as much as anyone, as the crime is very rare within their society.

Emergencies

Keep these numbers handy – **Rhodes General Hospital**:
☎ (0241) 22-222.
Tourist Police:
☎ (0241) 27-423.
Port Authority:
☎ (0241) 28-888.
Airport:
☎ (0241) 92-981/6.

Etiquette

In monasteries and churches, visitors are expected to dress with decorum: no shorts or bare tops for men; women should cover bare arms or legs so as not to cause offence. If you choose to ignore this advice, you may be refused admission to a place of worship.
Nudism is forbidden by law except in designated areas; topless sunbathing is permitted on most beaches.

Language

Greek is the main language of daily conversation, as well as on notices in shops and on signposts on the islands. Ferry destinations at ports are in Greek capitals. Pupils learn English at school, and many Greeks have worked in Germany and can speak a little German. Greek is a difficult language to master, but a few words of Greek will bring a warm response.

Useful Words
né • yes
ókhi • no
khérete • hello
ti kánete? • how are you?
adio • goodbye
parakaló • please
efkharistó • thank you
signómi • sorry/excuse me
póso iné? • how much is?
poté? • when?
pou? • where?
thélo • I'd like
aniktó • open
kleistó • closed
éna • one
dhío • two
tría • three
téssera • four
pénte • five
éxi • six
eftá • seven
okhtó • eight
enniá • nine
dhéka • ten

INDEX OF SIGHTS

GENERAL INDEX

GENERAL INDEX

94

GENERAL INDEX